ACKNOWLEDGEMENTS

I would like to thank the many talented people who assisted in the publication of this book for their contributions, guidance, and support. Without their editing, graphic design, and layout skills, this book would never have made it to market. Three cheers to the following: Merrikay Lee, Katie Tipton, Marianne Krcma, Jeff Phillips, Daniel DiPinto, and the professionals at Wordstop Technologies (P), Ltd.

I would also like to thank Jim Martin for writing the book *Free-Format RPG IV* (MC Press, May 2005). I used this book extensively when I learned how to code in free-format RPG.

Last, I'd like to show some love to the three individuals who mentored me when I was just starting out as programmer, fresh out of college. Combined, they are a big part of who I am professionally (although they may not want to admit that), and they remain in my life today. Many thanks to:

Jim Coker for his help with RPG, subfiles, and cramming a semester's worth of RPG homework assignments into one day, just before my final class. He was, and remains, my partner in crime in so many ways. . .literally. . .in fact, I have to stop right there.

Malcolm Niles for teaching me the basics of RPG and the workings of the System/34, and also for hiring me to moonlight for his consulting company back in the early days of my career. This experience not only helped me to become a better programmer but taught me a little about the consulting world and made me realize that personal computers still work without their covers.

Charles Fletcher for teaching me how the System/38 functioned, how it differed from the System/34, and how the RPG language changed to take advantage of its features. Charles also passed along many nuggets of wisdom, some pertinent to programming but most of them pertinent far beyond anything technical. He was Zen-like cool before anyone even knew what that meant. Oh, and I am pretty sure Charles invented the word "deselect" while writing a user manual in the early 1980s. That's how I see it, anyway.

CONTENTS

PREFACE

What could be more exciting than learning the cool subfile concepts and techniques provided in the first edition of this book? Learning more in this new edition, of course! Actually, subfile concepts haven't changed much from their inception in 1981, but the RPG language has changed, and changed drastically at that. Therefore, I felt it was time to update my previous book, *Subfiles in RPG IV*, to keep up with the new, hip version of RPG, as well as to take the opportunity to clean, tighten, and spit-shine, where needed. (Don't worry, no real spit was used in the creation of this book.)

The most significant change to the RPG language, and the focus of this edition, is the introduction of free-format RPG in the spring of 2001, with the release of V5R1. Yes, the publication of this book coincides with the tenth anniversary of free-format RPG! Although I use free-format RPG almost exclusively in the examples in this book, my purpose here is not to teach you how to use free-format RPG, nor to compare free format to its RPG predecessors. If you would like to learn more about free-format RPG on its own, Jim Martin's great book, *Free-Format RPG IV* (MC Press, 2005), provides everything you need to know about the latest, and definitely greatest, modification to the RPG language.

All that said, one advantage of free-format RPG is that it is easier to read than the prior versions of the language. So, even if you haven't coded much in free-format RPG, but are seasoned in one of the prior flavors of the language, you should be able to understand what is going on. That, combined with my excellent program documentation (ahem), should make understanding my code a piece of cake.

There are a few examples in this book that I decided to keep as they were in the previous edition, rather than rewrite for free-format RPG. Specifically, in Chapter 5, I kept the original RPG code instead of prototyping the message API call statements for free-format RPG. In Chapter 8, I also retained the original RPG code around the embedded SQL statements. Because there is no way to code embedded SQL in free-format RPG, I kept the RPG surrounding the embedded SQL statements in column-based RPG, so as not to confuse the issue . . . much like I may have confused the issue here in my explanation!

In addition to converting most of the original programs into free-format RPG, I also cleaned things up a little in this edition. Over the years, some "undocumented features" (errors) have been found in the code and text from the first edition. I took this opportunity to fix those things, and to generally rewrite and tighten some of the code from the first edition. In a few places, I realized that the free-format language enabled me to do things in new ways, so I decided to experiment a little, while keeping the original subfile-related content intact. How could I pass up a chance to use a For loop in RPG? Come on, you would have done the same thing. I also reread the whole book and added further explanations where I thought it necessary. (I just wanted you to know that, so you'd be impressed.)

I made a few other changes in the areas where I refer to the machine or the operating system. The term "OS/400" has been replaced with "IBM i" and "AS/400" with "System i." To be frank, I do not like the new names. I would have loved to stick with "OS/400" and "AS/400," but I had to roll with the times; however, if you happen to see one of these beloved terms in this book, do not consider it an error. Instead, know that it is my way of going "old school," showing you that some habits die hard.

Last, with this edition, you can view and download the complete source for all examples at *http://www.mc-store.com/5104.html*.

INTRODUCTION

You may ask yourself, "Why another book on subfiles? Have subfiles changed since their inception on the System/38, in 1981? Can't I read the IBM manuals and previously written subfile books and get along just fine?" Of course you can! The basic concepts of subfiles haven't changed much, and yes, you can read the IBM manuals and previously written materials to learn about subfiles.

"So what's with the new book?" you might ask. Well, even though the basic concepts of subfiles haven't changed much over the years, there have been some additions and improvements, including new Data Description Specifications (DDS) keywords and their related implementation techniques. Also, the language surrounding subfiles has changed drastically since those early days. The reconstruction of RPG in the form of RPG IV, along with the introduction of the Integrated Language Environment (ILE), has significantly changed how we create applications and has pushed the IBM midrange development environment closer to more of an object-oriented approach.

What follows from the changes to the system, to RPG, and to subfiles are new design fashions and programming techniques that must be consumed to fully take advantage of the environment, allowing us to create the best possible software solutions. A subset of this understanding is learning how to best employ subfiles in this modern environment. It's one thing to learn the basic concepts of subfile programming; it's quite another to learn how to program them in ways that allow them to work in harmony with today's surroundings. Reading previously written materials may satisfy part of the equation, but those resources won't teach you about what's new or about the most effective and efficient ways to incorporate subfile programming into today's development environment.

About This Book

So yes, this is another book on subfiles. But this one will provide you with the concepts, styles, and advanced topics of subfile programming, using RPG IV and ILE as its media. It will provide easy-to-understand explanations of subfile concepts, a bounty of practical examples, and some advanced techniques seldom seen in previous subfile books.

This book will take you on a journey from the very beginnings of subfile programming all the way to advanced techniques practiced by only those with a solid grasp of subfiles and the programming techniques and features of RPG IV and the ILE. More than simply getting you started with subfiles, it's meant to be a comprehensive resource that's used over and over again as you advance from very basic usage to guru-like practices.

This isn't a textbook—there are no exercises and exams at the end of each chapter to test what you've learned—but it certainly can be used as one. Each chapter builds upon the next so that you start with a solid base and build on that base as you proceed through the book. The purpose of this approach is to provide concepts, explanations, and practical examples you can use as templates for further development. The examples are available for download at *http://www.mc-store.com/5104.html*, so don't worry about having to rekey the code. Some basic knowledge of RPG IV and DDS is assumed. The contents of this book are there for the fine-tuning and enhancements of your skills.

What Does It Mean for Your Career?

Mastering subfiles has often been the defining moment in an RPG programmer's career. You might have been the best RPG II programmer in the world coming off the System/36, but if you didn't know subfiles, you were probably dismissed as an intermediate and told to "learn subfiles." Whether this is justifiable is another issue, but it's a widely accepted fact that until you know subfile programming, you can't say you're an expert.

When I interviewed for new jobs, the big question was always, "Do you know subfiles?" Not until I could confidently answer yes to that query and eagerly await the subfile-related questions that would surely follow did I know I had arrived. Armed with the formidable subfile power, I couldn't wait to go on interviews. Once hired as a programmer with subfile experience, I was looked at in an entirely new light.

This phenomenon is less apparent now for three reasons. First, subfiles have been around for many, many years now, and programmers entering the IBM i world today are being exposed to subfile programming. Second, the intervening years have swallowed up many a System/36 programmer, so there are mighty few programmers coming from a system where subfiles weren't available. Third, and most disturbing, is the *perception* that more RPG programmers know subfiles. I've worked in shops where this perceived knowledge spread throughout the programming staff like the plague. The problem was only partly the programmers' doing. They were assigned to programming projects that required subfiles and, using existing subfile programs as templates (as we've all done), would merrily code away. Well, simply cloning a subfile program doesn't make you *knowledgeable* in subfile programming. The other problem was with the code being used as a template. As you'll see later, there are a variety of subfile types, and each is used in a certain circumstance. Understanding this determination is paramount to writing good subfile programs.

What is still happening today in some shops is that the proper subfile techniques aren't being used in the correct circumstances. Worse still, there's some bad code out there, even if it is employing the appropriate technique. If someone clones a subfile program but doesn't know subfiles, he may not know it's bad or inappropriate code. Once he uses bad or inappropriate subfile code as a template, some people might assume he knows subfile programming when all he really knows is how to clone bad subfile programs. The proliferation of subfile programs in this manner can be hazardous to your IT shop's health.

Don't follow in that vein. Come learn some basic and advanced techniques for yourself so you can stop bad subfile programming in its tracks. And take the time to learn how to use subfiles with other IBM i tools such as recursion, data queues, and embedded SQL to create very powerful and efficient applications.

THE SPECIFICS ON SUBFILES

According to IBM, a subfile is a group of records that have the same record format and are read from and written to a display station in one operation. As this definition suggests, a subfile is not a file; rather, it is a temporary place to store data of the same format to be used by a display file program.

Why Use Subfiles?

Figure 1.1 shows the typical use of a subfile. As you can see, subfiles are useful when you want to list multiple, like records on a display. A major benefit of subfiles is that you can define them so the number of displayed records exceeds the number of lines available on the screen, allowing the user to scroll, or page, through the data. This is usually the reason you would decide to use subfiles in your display program. Because of their ease of use, however, I deploy subfiles even when I think I will never display more than one screen, because they are easy to change if the data someday requires more than one screen.

```
SFL001RG                Simple Subfile Program                 1/24/11
                                                               07:14:35


Last Name                First Name              MI    Nick Name
Baker                    Ana                     C     Abc
Bilog                    Frances                 X     Han Sing
Blade                    Billy                   B
Capacino                 Tony                    K     Knuckles
Fleischer                Jim                     R     Jimmy
Gandalf                  Norm                    A     Sammy
Hezikia                  Ezikiel                 U     Ezy
Jamison                  Antwain                 F     Anty
Jim                      Coker                   W     Bowling Stud
Joey                     Smite                   T     Fingahs
Jonas                    Steve                   W     Koolaid
Jones                    Jim                     S     Jim Jones
Jones                    Lennard                 C     Lenny
Kaplan                   Gabe                    T     Babe
Kekke                    Kenny                   K     Don't ask
Kelly                    Vandever                M     Pookie
Kent                     Craig                   S     Craig
                                                              More...

F3=Exit    F12=Cancel
```

Figure 1.1: A typical subfile application lists records from a file and allows the user to page through them.

In addition to simply displaying multiple lines of data, you can use subfiles and their multiple-line capabilities to add, change, and delete records very effectively. You can also use subfiles in a non-display manner, to create self-extending data structures and arrays in your RPG program. They work like multiple-occurrence data structures and arrays, except that instead of having to hard-code a number of elements large enough to hold the maximum number of entries, you can use subfiles. You start with a small number of entries and allow the number to expand dynamically, as your data expands.

Why Should You Care?

Haven't programmers been able to display data to a screen for years, without subfiles? Yes, but subfiles allow you to display lists of like data that can extend beyond one screen. They make it easier for you to create display applications, which, in turn, makes you more productive. Subfile programs are easy to write and maintain because much of the work is done for you in the Data Definition Specifications (DDS). Most of the time, you can change the characteristics of a subfile program without having to modify the RPG code driving it.

If that isn't enough, keep in mind that the ability to code subfiles is often the measure of an RPG programmer's worth. As an added benefit, when you're talking with a group of programmers at a users' group or technical conference, you can hold your head high, knowing that you're right up there with the rest of the subfile-savvy programmers.

Two DDS Formats Are Better Than One

As I stated earlier, most of the work in a subfile application is accomplished in the DDS. For every subfile you describe in your DDS, you're required to use two format types: a subfile record format (SFL) and a subfile control record format (SFLCTL). The subfile record format is used much as a record format is for a physical file. It defines the fields contained in a row of a subfile, describes the definition and attributes of those fields, and holds the actual data.

Unlike a physical file, however, a subfile record format is used only in memory, and only for the duration of the job. Once the program using the subfile ends, the data in that subfile is gone. Individual subfile records are read from, written to, and updated to the subfile by accessing the subfile record format in your program. The SFL keyword is required in your DDS to define a subfile record, just as the RECORD keyword is used for a typical display record format.

The subfile control record format describes the heading information for the subfile and controls how the subfile is going to perform. It's here that you define the size of the subfile, as well as the conditions under which the subfile will be cleared, initialized, displayed, and ended. The subfile control record format is unique because it controls aspects of a subfile in a way that other files aren't controlled. For example, you control the size of a physical file during compilation or by using the Change Physical File (CHGPF) command. You do not determine it in the DDS. Your program will operate the subfile control record format directly when it performs functions to the whole subfile, not individual records. Actions such as initializing, clearing, and displaying are accomplished in this fashion.

Four keywords are required in the subfile control record format:

1. The subfile control (SFLCTL) keyword identifies the subfile control record format, much as the record (RECORD) keyword identifies a typical display record format. The SFLCTL keyword also identifies the subfile record format that must immediately precede it.
2. The subfile size (SFLSIZ) keyword specifies the initial number of records the subfile may contain.
3. The subfile page (SFLPAG) keyword specifies the number of records that one screen of data may contain.
4. The subfile display (SFLDSP) keyword specifies when the subfile is displayed.

Note that the first requirement states that the SFLCTL keyword identifies the subfile record format that precedes it. Therefore, the SFL record format must immediately precede the SFLCTL format. The individual keywords available in each format can be placed in any order, but they must exist at the top of the format, before any constant or field definitions.

DDS and RPG Working as One

Once you code and compile the DDS for a subfile, you are ready to use that subfile in your RPG program. Your first three actions will be initializing, loading, and displaying your subfile. There are other things you can, and will, do to a subfile, but let's start with that foundation, and build up from there.

Before loading a subfile, you might want to clear or initialize it for use. Clearing or initializing takes effect when you write to the subfile control record format with the appropriate conditioning indicator set on, using the RPG WRITE operation. This isn't a requirement for the introductory load in your program, but as you create more complex subfile applications, you'll need to know the difference between clearing and initializing a subfile.

Let's return to the DDS for a moment. To clear a subfile, use the subfile clear (SFLCLR) keyword. This removes all records from the subfile. However, it does not remove them from the display until the next time the subfile is written to the screen by your program. This is different from the subfile initialize (SFLINZ) keyword, which will set all the records in your subfile to their default value. If you have no default value set in your DDS, numeric fields will default to zeros and character fields will default to blanks. Suppose your subfile size keyword is set to 100. If you clear it, instead of having an empty subfile, you will have 100 records, each initialized with its default value. I will talk more about SFLINZ later on, so don't worry if you don't quite get it yet. In short, the decision about whether to use SFLCLR or SFLINZ is determined by the role of your program.

You can load your subfile in a few different ways. The most common way is to retrieve data from one or more data files and write that data to the subfile record format, using the RPG WRITE operation. You might also choose to write only enough records to fit on one page (as determined by SFLPAG), and write more only if the user requests more; write all the desired records to the subfile before displaying the screen to the user; or use a combination of both. Still another way to load your subfile is to initialize the subfile first using the SFLINZ keyword, display the subfile with its default values to the screen, and allow the user to type data into the subfile from the screen.

As we go along in this book, I will show you examples of all these techniques because they are coded quite differently. I will also explain when to use which method.

Once your subfile is loaded or initialized, you're ready to display it. Depending on how you created your DDS, your subfile can take on many looks. No matter which form it takes, however, you only need one line of RPG code to display it.

Let's look at the code for a basic subfile program that displays a list of names. These could be the names of customers, salespeople, or employees; for our purpose, we'll just use generic names. Take notice of how much work is done with very little RPG code. Be careful, though. Once you understand this code, there's no turning back— you're on your way to becoming a subfile programmer.

Oh Goody! Some Code

The complete source for this example at is available at *http://www.mc-store.com/5104. html*, including compile information for a physical file (SFL001PF), a logical file (SFL001LF), a display file (SFL001DF), and the RPG (SFL001RG). To make this example work, you need to compile the three source members in order: first SFL001PF, then SFL001DF, and finally SFL001RG. In real life, it might not always matter whether you compile the data file before the display file, since the data file will probably already exist. In this example, however, I reference the physical file field information in my display file. As a result, the physical file needs to be created first. Figure 1.2 shows the code for the physical file.

```
A                                          UNIQUE
A          R PFR
A            DBIDNM        7 0
A            DBFNAM       20
A            DBLNAM       20
A            DBMINI        1
A            DBNNAM       20
A            DBADD1       30
A            DBADD2       30
A            DBADD3       30
A          K DBIDNM
```

Figure 1.2: The DDS for the physical file SFL001PF.

After creating the physical file, you'll need some sort of tool to get data into it. One way is to create a subfile program to enter the data, but that's what you'll learn later in this book. For now, you can use the IBM i operating system's (OS's) native Data File Utility (DFU) or any third-party package your shop already owns. To start DFU, run the command UPDDTA FILE(SFL001PF), or take Option 18 next to SFL001PF if you're using the Work with Objects Using Programming Development Manager (PDM) view.

The DDS for the physical file is pretty self-explanatory, so I will leave it alone. I'm going to start with the DDS for the display file. This is really where most of the work related to subfiles is accomplished. As I mentioned in the introduction, I'm assuming you have some basic knowledge of DDS. With that, let's jump to the subfile record format, signified by a record name of SFL1 and the record-level keyword of SFL. SFL1 is where you define the fields contained in each individual subfile record. It is also the format that will be written to in your RPG program. This is the format that will actually contain the subfile data.

The example in Figure 1.3 describes four fields: DBLNAM, DBFNAM, DBMINI, and DBNNAM. These fields are referenced from the physical file SFL001PF. It's important to notice here that these fields are defined as output only (indicated by the "O" in position 38), and they are set to start on row 5. That means the list of data to be displayed on the screen will start on row 5.

Each field has its own starting column number. DBLNAM starts in column 2, DBFNAM starts in column 26, and so on. The column settings let you place the fields across the row in whatever fashion you want, just as you would with a printed report. That's about it for the subfile record format.

```
A                                         DSPSIZ(24 80 *DS3)
A                                         PRINT
A                                         ERRSFL
A                                         CA03
A                                         CA12
A*
A           R SFL1                        SFL
A*
A             DBLNAM    R        O  5  2REFFLD(PFR/DBLNAM*LIBL/SFL001PF)
A             DBFNAM    R        O  5 26REFFLD(PFR/DBFNAM *LIBL/SFL001PF)
A             DBMINI    R        O  5 50REFFLD(PFR/DBMINI *LIBL/SFL001PF)
A             DBNNAM    R        O  5 55REFFLD(PFR/DBNNAM *LIBL/SFL001PF)
```

Figure 1.3: The DDS for the subfile record format SFL1 in SFL001DF.

You have defined your field's size and usage, and you have designed the layout of each field. The next record format is the subfile control record format, signified by the record name SF1CTL and the keyword SFLCTL. The subfile control format must come directly after the subfile record format. It's always distinguished by the SFLCTL keyword. Even though it has to come directly after the SFL format, you still must place the name of the subfile record format, in this case SFL1, within parentheses next to the SFLCTL keyword.

The DDS for SF1CTL is shown in Figure 1.4. The subfile record format is where you define everything about the individual record, while the subfile control record format is where you define everything about the subfile as a whole. You have two steps to take in the subfile control record format:

1. Define the subfile characteristics with a series of keywords.
2. Define any fields that will exist in the heading of the subfile.

The fields usually include column headings for the subfile records, as well as a title, program name, and date and time. However, they can also include input-capable fields, discussed in the next chapter. It's important to note that fields defined in the subfile control format are not part of the scrollable, subfile records.

```
A              R SF1CTL                    SFLCTL(SFL1)
A*
A                                          SFLSIZ(0500)
A                                          SFLPAG(0017)
A                                          OVERLAY
A N32                                      SFLDSP
A N31                                      SFLDSPCTL
A   31                                     SFLCLR
A   90                                     SFLEND(*MORE)
A                RRN1          4S 0H       SFLRCDNBR
A                                     4  2'Last Name'
A                                          DSPATR(HI)
A                                     4 26'First Name'
A                                          DSPATR(HI)
A                                     4 50'MI'
A                                          DSPATR(HI)
A                                     4 55'Nick Name'
A                                          DSPATR(HI)
A                                     1  2'SFL001RG'
A                                     1 27'Simple Subfile Program'
A                                          DSPATR(HI)
A                                     1 71DATE
A                                          EDTCDE(Y)
A                                     2 71TIME
```

Figure 1.4: The DDS for the subfile control record format SF1CTL in SFL001DF.

There is no requirement for the content of the fields in the subfile control record format, but there is a limit as to where they can be placed. Remember that the SFL record format started on row 5. That means that fields defined in the SFLCTL record format must not be placed anywhere below row 4. Now, looking at the example, let's examine the keywords used. They can be placed in any order within the SFLCTL record format, but they must also be entered before any fields or constants are defined.

The first thing I do in Figure 1.4 is define the subfile size (SFLSIZ) and subfile page size (SFLPAG). The SFLSIZ is set to 500. That means the initial number of records my subfile can contain is 500. I can extend the number contained in the SFLSIZ keyword up to a maximum of 9,999 records, but I will cover that in the next chapter.

The SFLPAG keyword determines how many records can fit on one page. I set mine to 17, meaning that each screen of data will contain a maximum of 17 records. You're limited on this parameter only by the number of records that can be physically displayed on a screen.

The OVERLAY keyword tells the display file to display the screen on top of what is already displayed—overlaying anything that is already there, but not erasing it. The subfile display (SFLDSP) keyword displays the subfile on the screen. It's conditioned, in this case, by N32, which means it will display only when indicator 32 is set off. You're not required to condition the SFLDSP keyword. I condition it in this example (and in most of my subfile programs, for that matter) because I want to stop the subfile from displaying if there are no records in it. You'll get a runtime error if you try to display a subfile with no records in it. There are a number of ways to handle the no-record situation, but I choose to set on indicator 32. This stops the subfile, and subsequent errors, from being displayed.

The next keyword is the subfile display control (SFLDSPCTL). This keyword allows you to display the control record format. The conditioning indicator on the SFLDSPCTL keyword, N31, conditions when the SFLCTL record format is to be displayed. In this case, the SFLCTL record format will be displayed only when it's told to do so by the RPG program, and when indicator 31 is off. This keyword isn't required if there are no fields to display or function keys to control in the format. Many keywords change the characteristics of the subfile, but these changes aren't seen until either the SFLDSP or the SFLDSPCTL keyword is activated.

The next keyword is the subfile clear (SFLCLR), which clears the subfile of its entries. It provides you with an empty subfile just waiting to have records written to it. Notice that I used the opposite conditioning indicator for the SFLDSPCTL keyword. I did this because the same RPG operation (WRITE) is used to display the control record format and clear the subfile. I probably don't want to clear the subfile at the same time I want to display it, so I use the same indicator. When indicator 31 is off, I want to display the subfile. When it's on, I want to clear it.

The subfile end (SFLEND) keyword tells the user there are more records in the subfile. A conditioning indicator is required when you're using the SFLEND keyword. In this case, indicator 90 conditions the SFLEND keyword. The *MORE parameter is just one of the valid parameters used with the SFLEND keyword. (The others will be discussed later.) It will cause the screen to show the word "More . . ." at the bottom-right corner of the last subfile record on the page. When the subfile is on its last page, the word "Bottom" replaces "More . . ." to indicate that this is the end of the subfile. SFLEND specified by itself, with no parameter, will cause the screen to display a plus sign ("+") in the lower-right corner when there are further pages to be displayed. When the subfile is on its last page, the plus sign is replaced by a blank.

Now that all the keywords have been defined, you can define any fields you need for your subfile control record format. In Figure 1.4, I describe some basic column headings: a title, the date, and the time. Because this is the same technique you would use to define headings on any display record format, it does not warrant discussion here.

Notice one particular field defined in the SFLCTL record format: RRN1, which will be used as my subfile relative record number. I define it as a 4-digit signed numeric, with no decimal places. (Remember that there is a maximum of 9,999 records in a subfile.) The "H" in position 38 indicates that this is a hidden field. I'm not going to display this field anywhere on the screen, but it's extremely important because it will keep track of which subfile record I'm working with.

The last record format defined in this DDS is the function key line. On line 23 of the display, I will list the function keys available to the user. This is the reason I use the OVERLAY keyword in the SFLCTL record format. I will first write the FKEY1 format, which will display on line 23, and then OVERLAY the FKEY1 format, but not erase it.

I use a separate record format to display the function keys because I want my function keys to appear at the bottom of the screen, as is standard with most IBM i display screens. I cannot place the function key constants in the subfile record format because I don't want them repeated with each subfile record. I'm also restricted from placing the function key constants in the subfile control format because doing so would violate the rule of the subfile control format not overlapping the subfile record format. The only way I could get away with placing the function key constants in the subfile control format is if I wanted them to display at the top of the screen. The FKEY1 format is shown in Figure 1.5.

```
A              R FKEY1

A*

A                           23   2'F3=Exit'

A                              COLOR(BLU)

A                           23 12'F12=Cancel'

A                              COLOR(BLU)
```

Figure 1.5: The DDS for function key record format FKEY1 in SFL001DF.

There, you have just learned how to build a basic subfile display file. This is more than a watered-down version appropriate only for learning. It is an example of a typical display file that you would actually use to display a list of data to a user. You've done the hard part, believe it or not. Now let's look at the RPG code necessary to load and display this subfile.

Figure 1.6 shows the file specifications (F specs). Notice that there are two files described. SFL001DF is the display file you just learned about. I define it as a combined (C in column 17), full procedural (F in column 18), externally described (E in column 22) workstation (WORKSTN) file. I further define SFL001DF on the next line of code by using the SFILE keyword with two parameters separated by a colon. The SFILE keyword defines a subfile contained in the display file. If you want to use that subfile in your program, you would code a SFILE line for every subfile record format contained in your DDS. The first parameter of the SFILE keyword is the name of the subfile record format, and the second is the field that will contain the subfile relative record number.

```
FSfl001df  cf    e                 Workstn

F                                  Sfile(Sfl1:Rrn1)

FSfl001lf  if    e         k Disk
```

Figure 1.6: RPG F specs for program SFL001RG.

Remember that I defined the relative record number field (RRN1) as a hidden field in the SFLCTL record format. The important thing to note is that the hidden field defined in the subfile record format is the one placed in the second parameter of the SFILE keyword. I will use SFL001LF, the logical file built over SFL001PF, to load the subfile.

The body of the program consists only of a main routine and one subroutine. The main routine, shown in Figure 1.7, is pretty simple. I first execute the subfile build routine (Build_Subfile) and then code the DOU loop that will process the screen until either the F3 or F12 key has been pressed. I set indicator 90 on before displaying the screen, so that the end of the subfile will be indicated properly. Indicator 90 is also the indicator I conditioned the SFLEND keyword on. Therefore, when the screen that contains the last record in the subfile is displayed, the word "Bottom" will appear in the lower-right corner.

```
/Free


  // Main Routine


  Exsr Build_Subfile;   // Execute the subfile build routine.


  Dou  *Inkc or *Inkl;  // Process until F3 or F12 is pressed.

    *In90 = *On;        // Set Subfile end indicator.

    Write Fkey1;        // Display the function key line.

    Exfmt Sf1ctl;       // Display the subfile.

  Enddo;


  *Inlr = *On;
```

Figure 1.7: The mainline code for RPG program SFL001RG.

Let's examine the Build_Subfile routine first, since that code will be executed before the DOU loop. The subroutine Build_Subfile is shown in Figure 1.8.

```
// ********************************************************************

// Build_Subfile - Build the List

// ********************************************************************



Begsr Build_Subfile;



// Clear the Subfile



Rrn1 = *Zero;        // Set the record counter to 0.

*In31 = *On;         // Turn on the subfile clear indicator.

Write Sf1ctl;        // Clear the subfile.

*In31 = *Off;        // Turn off the subfile clear indicator.



// Load data to subfile



Setll (*Loval) Sfl001lf;

Read Sfl001lf;
```

Continued

```
 Dow (Not %eof) And (Rrn1 <= 500); // Read while there are records in

                               // the file, up to the 500 limit.

  Rrn1 = Rrn1 + 1;  // Increment subfile record number.

  Write Sfl1;       // Write the record to the subfile.

  Read Sfl001lf;    // Read next data record.

Enddo;



// If no records were loaded, do not display the subfile



If Rrn1 = *Zero;    // If no records were loaded,

  *In32 = *On;      // set the indicator to NOT display the subfile.

Else;               // Otherwise,

  Rrn1 = 1;         // set the rec to 1 so the first page is displayed.

Endif;



Endsr;



/End-Free
```

Figure 1.8: The subroutine used to build the subfile in SFL001RG.

The first block of code clears the subfile (SFLCLR in the DDS). Because it was conditioned on indicator 31, I set on indicator 31 and write to the SFLCTL record format, which performs the clear. (The SFLDSPCTL isn't activated in this case because it's conditioned on indicator 31 being off.) After I write the SFLCTL record format, I set indicator 31 off, so the next write to the format will cause it to be displayed.

Now it's time to load data to the subfile. I do this by setting the file pointer to the beginning of the file and reading the first record of the data file. The three lines contained within the DOW loop are sufficient to load my subfile. I'm going to process the DOW loop until there are no more records in the file, or until I hit the 500-record limit set on the SFLSIZ keyword. Each time I read a record, I increment the subfile relative record number (RRN1) and write the record to the subfile record format. Because my subfile field names are the same as the data file field names, no MOVE, MOVEL, EVAL, or Z-ADD statements are necessary.

The IF statement below the loop keeps an error from ending the program. If no records were read from the file (RRN1 = 0), I set indicator 32 on. Remember that the subfile display (SFLDSP) keyword is conditioned on 32 being off. If it's on, the subfile won't be displayed. Displaying a subfile with zero records will cause an error and end the program.

Back in the main routine (Figure 1.7), now that the subfile is loaded, I will display it. Within the DOU loop, I write the function key format (FKEY1). This will display the function keys available to the user on line 23 of the screen. I then display the subfile with the execute format (EXFMT) keyword.

When displaying a subfile, the EXFMT is always done on the SFLCTL record format. Because the OS knows which subfile record format is associated with which subfile control record format, there's no need to explicitly perform an EXFMT to the SFL record format. I set indicator 31 off after the subfile was cleared, and with this write to the SFLCTL record format, the subfile control record will be displayed. If there are records in your subfile, indicator 32 will be off. As a result, the subfile should also be displayed.

Depending on how many records you added to your data file, you would see either "More . . ." or "Bottom" in the lower-right corner of the screen. If you saw "More . . . ," you'd be able to press the Page Down key to display the next page of data. You could do this until you saw "Bottom." If there were more than one page of data, you'd be able to use the Page Up key to scroll back to the top.

What's nice about this is that I didn't have to code a single line of RPG to handle the scrolling. IBM i took care of it for me. The program will sit on the EXFMT operation until a key is pressed that returns control back to the RPG program. In this case, the Page Up and Page Down keys are handled by the system and won't return control back to the program.

This method of subfile programming is called the *load-all* method. Using this method, you load the subfile one time, and display it to the screen. IBM i handles the paging for you. As you can see, it doesn't take a lot of code to get a load-all subfile up and running. In the next chapter, you'll learn more about the load-all method as well as two other methods, and when to use which one.

Hip Hop Subfiles Can Wrap

There might be a time when one line of data doesn't cut it. The subfile in Figure 1.1 displays first name, last name, middle initial, and nickname neatly on one line. But what if you want to show part of the address on the screen? There isn't enough room on the subfile line to squeeze in the address. What do you do? Do you abandon the subfile approach and try something else? The answer, thankfully, is no. With just a little more code in the DDS and, optionally, a couple more lines in the RPG, your subfile can display multiple lines of data per subfile record. Figure 1.9 shows the output from previous subfile programs, with the addition of the address, city, and state on a second line.

```
_SFL010RG               Simple Subfile Program                    1/17/11
                                                                 08:11:05


 Last Name            First Name              MI    Nick Name
 Baker                Ana                     C     Abc
    120 S. Kenilworth              Chicago, IL 88888
 Bilog                Frances                 X     Han Sing
    4444 North St.                 Lucky Town, USA
 Blade                Billy                   B


 Capacino             Tony                    K     Knuckles
    San Quentin                    Wherever San Quentin is
 Fleischer            Jim                     R     Jimmy
    820 Filler street              New Orleans, LA 87654
 Gandalf              Norm                    A     Sammy
    4444 Win Rd.                   Washington DC, 98765
 Hezikia              Ezikiel                 U     Ezy
    13 North St.                   Berlin, NH 99999
 Jamison              Antwain                 F     Anty


                                                                 More...


 F3=Exit    F11=Fold/Drop    F12=Cancel
```

Figure 1.9: An example of a subfile with lines that wrap.

Just Add the Fields

Most of the work needed to create the multiple-line subfile record is accomplished in the DDS. In fact, the only reason you might decide to modify the RPG is to tighten up the technique a little. You could easily leave the RPG alone and still provide multiple-line subfile records.

Figure 1.10 shows a new version of the subfile record format that places two address fields on a second line. All I've done is add two new fields on a second line of the subfile. The subfile starts on line 5 with the name fields, and now extends to a second line (line 6) with the addition of DBADD1 and DBADD2. This will cause your subfile to display two lines per record. The system figures all this out for you, once you define your subfile record format and determine how many records you want to display on a page (SFLPAG) in your record control format. You can see the complete DDS (SFL010DF) at *http://www.mc-store.com/5104.html*.

```
A              DBLNAM    R        O  5  2REFFLD(PFR/DBLNAM *LIBL/SFL001PF)
A              DBFNAM    R        O  5 26REFFLD(PFR/DBFNAM *LIBL/SFL001PF)
A              DBMINI    R        O  5 50REFFLD(PFR/DBMINI *LIBL/SFL001PF)
A              DBNNAM    R        O  5 55REFFLD(PFR/DBNNAM *LIBL/SFL001PF)
A              DBADD1    R        O  6  5REFFLD(PFR/DBADD1 *LIBL/SFL001PF)
A              DBADD2    R        O  6 37REFFLD(PFR/DBADD2 *LIBL/SFL001PF)
```

Figure 1.10: The subfile record format for a multiple-line subfile record.

This brings me to my next point. There is one additional step you'll have to take to properly fit this new subfile on the screen. You need to change the SFLPAG keyword in the control record format. In the previous example, SFLPAG was set to 17. However, trying to fit 17 double-lined subfile records on a page will create some problems when you try to compile. To counter this, you'll have to modify the SFLPAG number to some appropriate number. Because I had 17 before and am now displaying two lines per record, I changed the SFLPAG keyword to 8. That means the subfile will display eight two-line subfile records per page, which (and I know you can do the math) equates to 16 actual lines.

SFLFOLD and SFLDROP

By simply adding the two fields to the subfile record format, changing the SFLPAG keyword to 8, and recompiling both the display file and the RPG program, your subfile will now look something like Figure 1.9. Cool, right? Well, what if you want to toggle back and forth between one- and two-line subfile records? Maybe you don't always want to see the address information. Maybe you'd like to display the subfile as in Figure 1.1 and press a function key to show the address lines (Figure 1.9 shows that hint).

Is this asking too much? Of course not. With the addition of a few subfile keywords, you can actually toggle between single-line and multiple-line subfile records.

Figure 1.11 shows the additions to the subfile control format that make this happen. The SFLFOLD and SFLDROP keywords are used to toggle between displaying a full, multiple-line subfile record and its truncated, single-line version. Notice that Figure 1.11 uses both keywords in the subfile control format. I will explain why momentarily. First, let's talk about the difference between the two keywords.

```
A N10                                   SFLDROP(CA11)

A   10                                  SFLFOLD(CA11)

A                                       SFLMODE(&MODE)

A           MODE         1    H
```

Figure 1.11: Using SFLFOLD, SFLDROP, and SFLMODE together to switch between display modes.

Fold? Drop? Which Does Which?

Use SFLFOLD if you want to initially show the subfile in a folded format, displaying all the lines per subfile record. Use SFLDROP if you want to initially show the subfile in truncated form, where all but the first line in the subfile record is dropped. In parentheses, place the function key you want to use to toggle between folded mode and truncated mode. I used function key 11 (CA11).

Because this is a display-only subfile, I can use the Command Attention (CA) indicators, which do not transfer data back to your program when the function key is pressed. If this had been an input-capable subfile (something you'll see in Chapter 3), I would have wanted to use the Command Function (CF) indicator CF11 as the SFLFOLD or SFLDROP parameter. The CF indicator allows the data from the screen to transfer to your program when the function key is pressed.

Not Joined at the Hip

You can use either SFLFOLD or SFLDROP without necessarily having to use the other. For example, if you want to initially display the subfile in truncated form, but allow for multiple lines, you can use SFLDROP with CA11 as its parameter and not condition it on an indicator, as I did with N10 in Figure 1.11. This would start and display the subfile in truncated mode each time it's thrown to the screen from the program. Pressing F1 allows the user to switch to folded mode and view the subsequent data in each subfile record. However, once control is passed back to the program and the screen is again displayed, the subfile, because of the use of SFLDROP, is displayed in truncated mode.

Conversely, you can use SFLFOLD by itself with the CA11 parameter and no conditioning indicator in positions 9 and 10 to initially display the subfile in folded, or multiple-line, format. Again, by pressing F11, you can easily switch back and forth between truncated and folded mode, but once control is passed back to your program and the screen is thrown again, it will, because of the use of SFLFOLD, display in folded mode.

SFLFOLD and SFLDROP Working with SFLMODE

As you can see, you only need either SFLFOLD or SFLDROP to allow the user to switch back and forth between truncated and folded modes. So far, no changes have been made to the original RPG program for Figure 1.1 to make this happen. I suggest you try it out using one or the other to see how it works. However, you've probably already noticed from Figure 1.11 that I use both SFLFOLD and SFLDROP, and that I condition one on indicator 10 and the other on N10 (not 10). I like to do this because when control is passed back to my program and the subfile is thrown to the screen again, the subfile might change modes, possibly confusing users.

For example, if I use SFLDROP in my DDS, but press F11 to toggle to folded mode, the subfile will switch back to dropped mode when thrown to the screen again. Using both keywords and conditioning indicators stops this from happening. I can keep the subfile in one mode, regardless of whether control has passed back to the program, until I press F11 to change the mode.

SFLMODE tells the program which mode the subfile was in when control was passed back to it. If the subfile is in folded mode, SFLMODE will contain a zero; if it is in truncated mode, it will contain a one. If SFLMODE is used without SFLDROP or SFLFOLD, it will return a zero.

The &MODE parameter is the field that will contain the zero or one. It must be defined in the control record format as a one-byte hidden field. Notice the ampersand ("&") is used only in the parameter in the SFLMODE keyword, and not when actually defined. When control passes back to the program, I can tell the program which mode the subfile is in and ensure that it's thrown to the screen in that same mode.

A Little RPG Never Hurt Anyone

The last step to my kicked-up SFLFOLD/SFLDROP technique is to add a little code to the RPG program, shown in Figure 1.12. After the EXFMT operation, when control is returned to the program, I check the mode and set indicator 10 appropriately. If the mode is zero or *OFF, which means the subfile was in folded mode, I set indicator 10 on. That way, when the subfile is displayed again, it is displayed in folded mode. If the mode is one, which means the subfile was in truncated mode, I set 10 off (N10). This ensures that the subfile is displayed in truncated mode the next time it is thrown to the screen. You can find the complete RPG code for the SFL001RG program at *http://www. mc-store.com/5104.html*.

```
If Mode = *On;        // This code is used to "stick" the mode.

   *In10 = *Off;      // Remove this If block if you would like

Else;                 // the ENTER key to also toggle the format.

   *In10 = *On;

Endif;
```

Figure 1.12: This code enables the subfile mode to "stick" when the subfile is redisplayed.

A Little Work Goes a Long Way

By using SFLFOLD, SFLDROP, and SFLMODE together, I have not really done anything that can't be done by using either SFLDROP or SFLFOLD by itself without SFLMODE and the RPG modifications. What I have done is provide the user with a more consistent display and, because the mode will only change if the F11 key is pressed, more control. In my opinion, it's worth the little extra work.

The Last Word on SFLFOLD and SFLDROP

SFLFOLD and SFLDROP can only be used when SFLPAG and SFLSIZ aren't equal. If SFLPAG and SFLSIZ are equal (something we'll look at in the next chapter), SFLFOLD and SFLDROP are ignored. Also, when you're using both keywords in a subfile control format, they must both use the same function key as a parameter. It's a requirement.

The Fine Print

Before we go on, let's take a look at the DDS keywords and RPG operations you can use with subfiles. As you go along in this book, you'll see an example of most of the DDS keywords listed in Tables 1.1 and 1.2, and all of the RPG operations in Table 1.3. In some cases, I simply mention where a keyword might be used and what it will do, leaving it up to you to modify any chapter's program or programs for use with that keyword. Having said that, however, I tried to provide an example of each keyword, unless it just didn't make sense to create a whole new program for it.

Note that only a smattering of what's available was used in the examples you've seen so far. That's okay—and normal. I have never written a subfile program that used all the available DDS keywords and RPG operations. In most cases, I use only a few. Which few I use depends on what I am trying to accomplish at the time. Note also that you may use other, non-subfile keywords when defining your subfile. I used the OVERLAY keyword in my example. The tables below contain only subfile-specific keywords. Finally, note that most of the DDS keywords mentioned in the tables below are subfile specific, whereas only one RPG operation code is subfile-specific.

Table 1.1: Subfile Control Record Keywords (SFLCTL)	
Keyword	**Description**
SFLCLR	Clears the subfile of all records
SFLMSG	Used for subfile messages
SFLDLT	Deletes the subfile
SFLMSGID	Used for subfile message identifications
SFLDROP	Enables a command key to fold or truncate subfile records
SFLPAG	Controls the number of records to display on one page (screen) of data
SFLDSP	Controls when the subfile is displayed

Keyword	Description
SFLRCDNBR	Displays the page of a subfile based on the subfile record number
SFLDSPCTL	Controls when the subfile control record is displayed
SFLRNA	Allows for nonactive subfile records
SFLEND	Tells the users if they are at the end of a subfile or if there are more records to display
SFLROLVAL	Rolls records by a specified number instead of by page
SFLENTER	Enables the Enter key to work as the Page Up key
SFLRTNSEL	Returns all selections chosen in a selection list when asked by the RPG program
SFLFOLD	Enables a command key to fold or truncate subfile records
SFLSCROLL	Returns to relative record number of the record at the top of the current page
SFLINZ	Initializes subfile records to their default values
SFLSIZ	Specifies the size of the subfile
SFLLIN	Specifies the number of spaces between subfile records located on the same line
SFLSNGCHC	Defines a single-choice selection list
SFLMLTCHC	Defines a multiple-choice selection list
ROLLUP	Allows the ability to scroll through the data (same as PAGEDOWN)
PAGEDOWN	Allows the ability to scroll through the data (same as ROLLUP)
ROLLDOWN	Allows the ability to scroll back through the data (same as PAGEUP)
PAGEUP	Allows the ability to scroll back through the data (same as ROLLDOWN)

Table 1.1: Subfile Control Record Keywords (SFLCTL) (Continued)

Keyword	Description
SFL	Identifies the subfile record format
SFLMODE	Determines whether the subfile was in folded or truncated mode
SFLCHCCTL	Controls the availability of choices in a selection list
SFLMSGKEY	Allows a subfile to contain messages from a program message queue
SFLCSRPRG	Specifies the cursor progression for a subfile
SFLMSGRCD	Also allows a subfile to contain messages from a program message queue
SFLCSRRRN	Determines where the cursor is located within the subfile
SFLNXTCHG	Returns the next changed subfile record when asked by the RPG program
SFLCTL	Identifies the subfile control record format
SFLPGMQ	The third in the trilogy of subfiles and program message queues, along with SFLMSGKEY and SFLMSGRCD

Table 1.2: Subfile Record Keywords (SFL)

Table 1.3: RPG Operation Codes Used with the Subfile Control Record Format (SFLCTL)	
Op Code	**Description**
WRITE	Controls the subfile control record format
EXFMT	Displays the subfile to the screen and waits for a response from the user
READ	Reads from the subfile control record format

Table 1.4: RPG Operation Codes Used with the Subfile Record Format (SFL)	
Op Code	**Description**
WRITE	Writes to the subfile record format
CHAIN	Gets a subfile record by relative record number
UPDATE	Updates the contents of a subfile record
READC	Reads the next changed record from a subfile

Subfile Trivia for That Special Moment

A maximum of 24 subfiles can be active at any one time. A maximum of 12 subfiles can be displayed on the base screen or in a single window at any one time. I can't tell you how many times I've used this information to wow colleagues at work and impress friends at social gatherings. Actually, I can tell you—never! However, I would be wowed and impressed if someone came up with a valid application where these numbers were too limiting (remember that I said "valid").

Summary

The following is a list of the subfile keywords and some important concepts you should take from this chapter:

- The subfile control record format (SFLCTL) handles the whole subfile, whereas the subfile record format (SFL) handles individual subfile records.
- Most of the work in a subfile is done in the DDS and by the operating system.
- With just a few RPG operations, most of which you already know, you can process subfiles in your program.
- The four required DDS keywords are SFL, SFLCTL, SFLSIZ, and SFLPAG.
- SFLFOLD and SFLDROP are used to toggle between a display of a full, multiple-line subfile record and its truncated, single-line version.

2

A Subfile Type
for Every Occasion

As you've learned, there are three types of subfiles. The subfile used in Chapter 1 was a load-all subfile, which allows the records to be loaded to the subfile at one time, before the subfile is displayed. What makes this program a load-all subfile is that IBM i handles the paging for you, and all your records are displayed at the beginning of the program, before the data is displayed to the user. There's no code in your RPG program to allow you to page up or down through your subfile. You have only one routine that loads all the data from your data file until either the end-of-file is reached or the maximum number of allowed records (500 in this example) is reached.

This type of subfile is very easy to code and can allow you to get a working application up and running rather quickly. It's great if you're certain about the number of records you want to display. Because the OS handles the paging for you, you can just load and display. The user can page through the data, and you don't even code for it in your RPG.

However, if something seems too good to be true, it probably is. The problem with load-all subfiles comes when the amount of data increases. Maybe there are more records that need to be loaded. The program will not blow up—we've coded for that in the DOW loop—but the data will not display.

I could modify the DDS and set the SFLSIZ keyword as high as 9,999, and then go into the RPG program and change the SUBFILE_SIZE constant to match the SFLSIZ keyword.

Now all the data will be loaded—as long as the number of records doesn't exceed 9,999. But what about the poor users who have to scroll through seemingly endless pages of data to find what they're looking for? That's another potential problem with the load-all subfile program and IBM i: controlled paging. Scrolling through several pages of data can be time-consuming, especially if the desired data is close to the bottom of the list.

One last pitfall to the load-all technique is the potential performance implications incurred when so much data is loaded at one time. Not only does it take some time to load thousands of records to a subfile, but the task also requires a considerable amount of system resources.

You have to be careful, therefore, when using the load-all technique. You have to balance how many records you want to display, how many potential pages you want the user to page through, and the potential performance issues of loading the data involved.

Let's say you are not sure how many records will be displayed, or you know the number, but it's relatively high (for example, 1,000 records). How do you best write a subfile program that displays all the records, but also allows the user easy access? You do this by using the second of the three subfile types: self-extending subfiles.

Self-Extending Subfiles

Because you still can't load more than 9,999 records (this is a not-so-subtle hint that there might be a way to load more than 9,999), the self-extending subfile works the same as a load-all subfile. However, it differs in a couple of other ways. A self-extending subfile allows the user to add records to the subfile only when they are needed. Normally, this is done one page at a time, although it doesn't have to be. By loading only a specified amount of data at a time, the self-extending subfile's performance will be more consistent than a load-all subfile, which might load 50 records one time and 500 records the next. Another advantage is that by using a self-extending subfile and a position-to technique, you can make navigation within the subfile more flexible.

Let's look at the DDS and the RPG program for this technique, and compare them to the load-all technique discussed earlier. (The complete DDS and RPG for the programs used here can be found at *http://www.mc-store.com/5104.html*. I'll be showing you only the parts of the code that are pertinent or different from previous examples.) First, let's take a gander at the DDS. SFL002DF looks much like the load-all DDS, with a few changes. Figure 2.1 shows the subfile control record from the DDS, which is the only part of the DDS that has any changes.

```
A            R SF1CTL               SFLCTL(SFL1)

A*

A                                   SFLSIZ(0016)

A                                   SFLPAG(0015)

A                                   OVERLAY

A                                   ROLLUP(27)

A N32                               SFLDSP

A N31                               SFLDSPCTL

A  31                               SFLCLR

A  90                               SFLEND(*MORE)

A            RRN1       4S OH       SFLRCDNBR

A                              6  2'Last Name'

A                                   DSPATR(HI)

A                              6 26'First Name'

A                                   DSPATR(HI)
```

Continued

```
A                                6 50'MI'

A                                  DSPATR(HI)

A                                6 55'Nick Name'

A                                  DSPATR(HI)

A                                1  2'SFL002RG'

A                                1 71DATE

A                                  EDTCDE(Y)

A                                2 71TIME

A                                1 24'Subfile Program with Position To'

A                                  DSPATR(HI)
```

Figure 2.1: The DDS control file record for a self-extending subfile (SFL002DF).

Notice that I changed the SFLSIZ from 500 to 16. This doesn't really mean much because both the load-all and self-extending subfiles require that the SFLSIZ be greater than the SFLPAG. Where it really matters is in how you load the subfile in your RPG code. I could have used 500 here, too, but my standard for self-extending subfiles is to make SFLSIZ one greater than SFLPAG and only load one page of records at a time in my RPG program.

Next, notice that I added the ROLLUP keyword. This will allow my RPG program to control when more records are added to the subfile. With a self-extending subfile, it's important to note that the duties of paging through the data will be shared by your RPG program and the OS. Adding the ROLLUP keyword tells IBM i that whenever the last page of the subfile is displayed and the user presses the Page Down key, the program will take control and handle the paging. When the user isn't on the last page, or is paging back through the data, IBM i will handle the paging. You will see more about this in the discussion of the RPG code.

Now that we've seen that the DDS needed only a few changes to become a self-extending subfile, let's glance at the RPG program (SFL002RG) and see what's going on there. Figure 2.2 shows the F and D specs for the program.

```
FSf1002df  cf  e            Workstn

F                                   Sfile(Sfl1:Rrn1)

F                                   Infds(Info)

FSf10011f  if  e         k Disk


DSflpag        C                    Const(15)


DLstrrn        S            4  0 Inz(0)

Di             S            4  0 Inz(0)
```

Figure 2.2: The standard F and D specs for a subfile program (SFL002RG).

Notice that the specs include a stand-alone field called LSTRRN. This field will be used to contain the last relative record number written to the subfile during the subfile load routine. When the user presses the Roll Up key, the program will know where in the subfile to start writing records.

Notice also that I have separated the clearing of the subfile from the loading of the subfile, by placing the tasks in two separate subroutines. I do this in a self-extending subfile program because I don't want to clear the subfile every time I load records.

Because I'm going to add records to the subfile when the user presses the Roll Up key, I don't want to clear it first. We'll get to the mainline of the program in a moment, but first let's look at the clear subfile routine, shown in Figure 2.3.

```
Begsr Clear_Subfile;



Rrn1 = *Zero;          // Clear the subfile record number.

Lstrrn = *Zero;        // Clear the saved subfile record number.

*In31 = *On;           // Set the indicator to clear the subfile.

Write     Sflctl;      // Clear the subfile.

*In31 = *Off;          // Turn OFF the clear subfile indicator.

*In32 = *Off;          // Set the indicator to display the subfile.

*In90 = *Off;          // Turn off the subfile end indicator.



Endsr;
```

Figure 2.3: The clear routine for a self-extending subfile (SFL002RG).

In the Clear_Subfile subroutine, I set both the relative record number (RRN1) and the last relative record number (LSTRRN) to zero. I'll use LSTRRN to hold the last relative record of the subfile, so that when I add records to the subfile, I'll know where I left off.

After setting on indicator 31, which conditions the SFLCLR keyword, I write to the subfile control record format to clear the subfile. Then I set off indicator 31, which conditions the SFLDSPCTL keyword, and set off indicator 32, which conditions the SFLDSP keyword. Lastly, I set off the SFLEND indicator, 90.

The subfile load routine shown in Figure 2.4 is a little different from the one for the load-all subfile. This is mainly because I'm only going to load one page of data at a time, not all the available records from my database file. In this case, field SFLPAG is set as a constant in my D specs and will contain the same number as the SFLPAG keyword in DDS. If you decide to change the keyword in the DDS, you'll have to change the D spec in your RPG. Don't let the fact that they have the same name fool you. I just like doing it that way.

```
Begsr Build_Subfile;


Rrn1 = Lstrrn;        // Set the current relative record number

                      // equal to the last saved relative record

                      // number so that the subfile will load

                      // correctly.

For i = 1 to Sflpag;  // Load subfile with one page of data.

  Read Sfl0011f;

  If %eof;            // If end of file is reached,

    *In90 = *On;      // set subfile end indicator on.

    Leave;            // Leave the For loop.

Endif;
```

Continued

```
   Rrn1 = Rrn1 + 1;     // Increment the subfile record number.

   Write Sfl1;          // Write the data record to the subfile.

 Endfor;




 If Rrn1 = *Zero;       // If no records were written to the subfile,

   *In32 = *On;         // turn on the indicator to NOT display the

 Endif;                 // subfile.




 Lstrrn = Rrn1;         // Save the last record number for the next

                        // page build.

 Endsr;




/End-Free
```

Figure 2.4: The load routine for a self-extending subfile (SFL002RG).

If end-of-file is reached, indicator 90 will come on, and the routine will exit the FOR loop. Indicator 90 also conditions SFLEND. Otherwise, the routine increments the relative record by one and writes to the subfile record format. Once the loop has finished its work by either writing the prescribed number of records to the subfile (17, in this case) or hitting end-of-file, it checks to determine whether to display the subfile by conditioning indicator 32 and then sets LSTRRN appropriately.

Now, let's go back to the main routine, where you'll see a more complex DOU loop than that contained in the load-all subfile. Figure 2.5 shows the mainline code.

```
/Free


// Main Routine


Exsr Clear_Subfile;    // Execute the subfile clear routine.

Exsr Build_Subfile;    // Execute the subfile build routine.


Dou   *Inkc or *Inkl;    // Process until F3 or F12 is pressed.

  Write Fkey1;           // Display the function key line.

  Exfmt Sf1ctl;          // Display the subfile.


  Select;                // Process data entered by the user.


    When (Cfkey = *In27) And (Not *In32);

      Exsr Build_Subfile; // Execute the subfile build routine.



  Endsl;


Enddo;


*Inlr = *On;
```

Figure 2.5: The mainline routine for a self-extending subfile (SFL002RG).

This isn't very complex. I've added code to handle the Roll Up key to the original load-all mainline. Remember that I used 27 with the ROLLUP keyword in the DDS, which means that when the Page Down (Roll Up) key is pressed, indicator 27 will be set on. If indicator 27 is on, and the subfile isn't empty (*IN32 is off), the code simply executes the Build_Subfile subroutine, which will add to the subfile from where it left off, without clearing it. (Note: I have tried to be consistent with term use, but when discussing the finer points of maneuvering through a subfile, I use the terms *page down* and *roll up* interchangeably. These terms are synonymous, as are *page up* and *roll down*.)

Let's go back to the EXFMT command for a minute. Remember that with a self-extending subfile, paging duties are shared between your program and the OS. This is where that decision takes place. Your program will sit on this line of code until a valid function key (as defined in your DDS) or the Enter key is pressed. However, when the Page Down key is pressed, IBM i is smart enough to know whether it's about to page through data already in the subfile, in which case it can handle the operation. If the last page of the subfile is already displayed, IBM i knows to pass control back to your program.

IBM i always handles the page-up (roll-down) duties in a self-extending subfile. Basically, this means when you call your program for the first time, the first page of data will be displayed. If you press the Page Down key to get more records, control will pass back to your program, and 17 more records will be written to the subfile. Now there will be 34 records in your subfile, and the second page (records 18 through 34) will be displayed. If you press Page Up to get back to the first page of data, IBM i will navigate that one for you and, because those records already exist in the subfile, your program will do nothing. If you decide to page-down again to get to the second page, IBM i will also handle that, since records 18 through 34 already exist. If you decide to see a third page—you guessed it—control is passed to your program to add 17 new records to your subfile.

The self-extending subfile is probably the most widely used type of subfile. It balances nicely between letting IBM i handle a bit of the processing and allowing you to add some code to increase flexibility for the user.

Add Some Oomph

Now that you have the self-extending basics down, let's look at some techniques to make your subfile programs more flexible for the user, and easier to code and understand for the programmer.

One thing I like to do in my subfile programs is give the user an additional navigation tool. It could get tedious, for instance, if a user is interested in a name beginning with "V," and the file contains thousands of names listed in alphabetical order. It would be nice if the user could position to the names starting with "V," and page from there. Better yet, if the user knows the exact name, he could position to that location without paging at all. The position-to field allows that flexibility. It isn't required, but I always use it in the subfile control record format whenever I create a subfile. To me, writing a subfile program without position-to capabilities is like being forced to stop on every floor of a high-rise building, even if you live on the top floor.

The position-to field enables the user to navigate directly to a specific position in a subfile. For example, suppose the "A"s in a name list are displayed. You could enter a name, or partial name, starting with "Z" in the position-to field, and the subfile would position to the "Z"s, or the name closest to "Z" if there were none in the file.

Let's take another look at the subfile control format from SFL002RG. This time, I've added a position-to field called PTNAME. Figure 2.6 shows the pumped-up control record format.

```
A           R SF1CTL                    SFLCTL(SFL1)
A*
A                                       SFLSIZ(0016)
A                                       SFLPAG(0015)
A                                       OVERLAY
A                                       ROLLUP
A N32                                   SFLDSP
A N31                                   SFLDSPCTL
A 31                                    SFLCLR
A 90                                    SFLEND(*MORE)

                                                        Continued
```

```
A                RRN1          4S 0H    SFLRCDNBR
A                                       6 2'Last Name'
A                                       DSPATR(HI)
A                                       6 26'First Name'
A                                       DSPATR(HI)
A                                       6 50'MI'
A                                       DSPATR(HI)
A                                       6 55'Nick Name'
A                                       DSPATR(HI)
A                                       1 2'SFL002RG1'
A                                       1 71DATE
A                                       EDTCDE(Y)
A                                       2 71TIME
A                                       1 24'Subfile Program with Position To'
A                                       DSPATR(HI)
A                                       4 2'Position to Last Name . . .'
A                PTNAME       20 B      4 30CHECK(LC)
```

Figure 2.6: The subfile control format with the position-to field PTNAME (SFL002DF).

To make room for the position-to field, I changed the SFLPAG keyword from 17 to
15. In keeping with my standard of assigning SFLSIZ as one greater than SFLPAG for
self-extending subfiles, I also set SFLSIZ to 16. This makes room for the position-to
field, PTNAME, on line 4 of the screen. I define it as a 20-byte field, which matches the
field length for the LAST NAME field in the data file. The "B" in position 38 allows the
user to make an entry in the field. The CHECK keyword with the LC parameter allows
lowercase characters.

In the RPG program, the only additional logic necessary is a when block in the mainline routine to determine whether something is entered in the position-to field. If something is entered, the program needs to do the following:

- Clear the subfile by executing the Clear_Subfile routine.
- Position the data file with a SETLL operation using the PTNAME field.
- Load the subfile by calling the Build_Subfile routine.
- Clear the PTNAME field before displaying the subfile to the screen.

Figure 2.7 shows an example of the block of code you might use for this. No matter where you are in your subfile, the subfile will be cleared when you enter something in the PTNAME field, and 15 new records will be written and displayed, based on what was entered.

```
When (Cfkey = Enter) And (Ptname <> *Blanks);

  Setll (Ptname) Sfl0011f;

  Exsr Clear_Subfile; // Execute the subfile clear routine.

  Exsr Build_Subfile; // Execute the subfile build routine.

  Clear Ptname;        // Clear the position-to field.
```

Figure 2.7: The mainline logic to handle the position-to field (SFL002RG).

Figures 2.8 and 2.9 show what happens when the position-to field is used. Figure 2.8 shows the file beginning with the last name "Anthony." To position the file to "Vandever," simply type that into the position-to field and press Enter. The list will be repositioned, as shown in Figure 2.9.

```
SFL002RG              Subfile Program with Position To           1/24/11
                                                                 07:39:24

Position to Last Name . . . Vandever_____

Last Name              First Name           MI   Nick Name
Anthony                Tony                 A    Bill
Baker                  Ana                  C    Abc
Bilog                  Frances              X    Han Sing
Blade                  Billy                B
Capacino               Tony                 K    Knuckles
Fleischer              Jim                  R    Jimmy
Gandalf                Norm                 A    Sammy
Hezikia                Ezikiel              U    Ezy
Jamison                Antwain              F    Anty
Jim                    Coker                W    Bowling Stud
Joey                   Smite                T    Fingahs
Jonas                  Steve                W    Koolaid
Jones                  Jim                  S    Jim Jones
Jones                  Lennard              C    Lenny
Kaplan                 Gabe                 T    Babe
                                                          More...

F3=Exit    F12=Cancel
```

Figure 2.8: A subfile example involving a list of names.

```
SFL002RG              Subfile Program with Position To           1/24/11
                                                                 07:40:18

Position to Last Name . . . _____

Last Name              First Name           MI   Nick Name
Vandever               Corina               R    Wine Diva
Vandever               Felicia              R    Fish
Vandever               Kalia                M    Smiley
Vandever               Kevin                M    Subfile Man
Zak                    Bob                  T    Zak

















                                                          Bottom

F3=Exit    F12=Cancel
```

Figure 2.9: The list of names repositioned to the name "Vandever."

Even More Oomph

There's one last technique to look at before we move on: a better way to handle the Enter and function keys in your program. Take a look back at Figure 2.5, and you'll see that the F3, F12, and Roll Up keys are represented by *INKC, *INKL, and *IN27, respectively. These aren't very intuitive labels, which makes it difficult for someone to follow what's going on in the code. You might also notice that the Enter key isn't represented at all. There's no keyword entry in DDS for the Enter key, and no indicator to associate with it. Therefore, it's common in a display program to assume that Enter has been pressed only after all the other valid function and page keys have been checked.

This isn't the most efficient way to process the display program, especially since Enter is the key that is pressed most often. Wouldn't it be nice if you could provide more descriptive names for the function keys, as well as include a way to process the Enter key explicitly, before the other keys are checked? Well, you can do just that by including the file information data structure in your program and using the attention-indictor byte from the data structure to determine which key has been pressed.

Just a few changes are needed to our self-extending subfile to incorporate this new technique. The only change you need to make in the DDS is to remove the parameter 27 from the ROLLUP keyword. You no longer need to associate an indicator with ROLLUP.

Let's take a look at additions to the RPG program. Figure 2.10 shows how to define the attention-indicator byte. Notice the addition of D specs and an extra F spec. The

```
FSfl002df  cf   e              Workstn

F                                 Sfile(Sfl1:Rrn1)

F                                 Infds(Info)

FSfl0011f  if   e      k Disk




DInfo            ds

                                                    Continued
```

```
D Cfkey                     369    369


DExit            C                      Const(X'33')

DCancel          C                      Const(X'3C')

DEnter           C                      Const(X'F1')

DRollup          C                      Const(X'F5')

DSflpag          C                      Const(15)


DLstrrn          S                   4  0 Inz(0)

Di               S                   4  0 Inz(0)
```

Figure 2.10: The F and D specs for the file information data structure with an attention-indicator byte (SFL002RG).

additional F spec defines a data structure (INFO) as the file information data structure for the display file SFL002DF. In the D specs, notice that the INFO data structure contains only one field, CFKEY. The file information data structure contains all kinds of data about its associated file, but I'm only interested in one byte of it. When the user presses a valid key and control returns back to the RPG program, CFKEY contains a hexadecimal representation of the key pressed.

I next set up constants to define more meaningful names to the hexadecimal values. Now, instead of using INKC to condition code when F3 is pressed, I can use the word "exit." (You'll see what I mean as we get into the code.) Please note that the new F and D specs are not specific to subfiles. If you already have a method of processing display files, use it. I just want to share my programming techniques with you, even if they're not related specifically to subfiles.

Figure 2.11 shows the addition of the position-to field and the new constants to the original self-extending mainline routine. Notice the first use of the CFKEY value. After writing the function key line and throwing the subfile as you've seen before, a SELECT routine handles the possible responses from the user. I like to use SELECT and WHEN clauses because they make my programs more modular, and therefore easier to read. Once a WHEN clause is satisfied, the remaining clauses are ignored. As a result, it makes sense to validate the keys in the order of their potential use. If you think Enter is going to be pressed most often, check for it in your first WHEN clause. One of the advantages of the attention-indicator byte is that it allows you to specifically check for the Enter key.

The responses I care about in the SELECT logic are Enter, Roll Up, F3, and F12. When Enter is pressed, the code also checks whether data has been typed into the position-to field, PTNAME. If it has, that data will be used to position the file with a SETLL operation. Then, the code will execute the Clear_Subfile routine, load the subfile based on the position-to entry, and, finally, clear the position-to field (PTNAME) before displaying the subfile again.

```
/Free


   // Main Routine



   Exsr Clear_Subfile;   // Execute the subfile clear routine.

   Exsr Build_Subfile;   // Execute the subfile build routine.



   Dou  *Inkc or *Inkl;   // Process until F3 or F12 is pressed.

     Write Fkey1;         // Display the function key line.
```

Continued

```
   Exfmt Sf1ctl;              // Display the subfile.



   Select;                    // Process data entered by the user.


  When (Cfkey = Enter) And (Ptname <> *Blanks);

    Setll (Ptname) Sf1001lf;

    Exsr Clear_Subfile; // Execute the subfile clear routine.

    Exsr Build_Subfile; // Execute the subfile build routine.

    Clear Ptname;       // Clear the position-to field.


  When (Cfkey = Rollup) And (Not *In32);

    Exsr Build_Subfile; // Execute the subfile build routine.


  Endsl;



Enddo;


*Inlr = *On;
```

Figure 2.11: The mainline code using the new techniques.

Notice how the attention-indicator byte is used to explicitly process Enter, which is typically the most-used key. Also notice how much easier the code is to read now that ROLLUP instead of *IN27 is used for the Roll Up key, enter is used for the Enter key, exit for the F3 key, etc.

Again, the use of the attention-indicator byte from the file information data structure and a position-to field are not required in a subfile program. I introduce these techniques because I use them throughout the rest of the book, as well as in all of my actual subfile applications. I believe it's valuable information as you learn to code display programs. Now, let's get back to subfiles.

Page-at-a-Time Subfiles

The page-at-a-time subfile is yet a third type of subfile. While it requires a little more coding, it provides more flexibility to the user. The theory behind the page-at-a-time subfile is that you never have more than one page of data in your subfile at a time. The primary advantage of this type of subfile is that you aren't restricted to the 9,999-record limit of the load-all and self-extending subfiles.

Because the subfile is cleared and reloaded when each page key is pressed (up or down), you can page through an infinite number of records. I've created a second advantage by adding a position-to field. Because you reload the subfile with each page key pressed, you can now page up from the beginning of a subfile list (as long as it's not the beginning of your data file).

With the self-extending subfile, if you used the position-to field, the data keyed into the position-to field determined the top of your list. The only way to get the previous data was to use the position-to field again. With the page-at-a-time subfile, when you use the position-to field, you can page up from the top of the list to get to previous data. This is because your program will handle both paging up and paging down. This type of subfile offers the most user flexibility, but it also requires the most code and can be the most performance-intensive.

Figure 2.12 shows the subfile control record for a page-at-a-time subfile (SFL003DF). Notice that there are only two changes from a self-extending subfile. The first is that SFLPAG and SFLSIZ are the same. This means that your subfile will never contain more than one page of data. (If you attempt to load past the amount specified in SFLSIZ, you will get an error—so don't do that.) The second change is the addition of the ROLLDOWN keyword. This tells IBM i that your RPG program will now handle all the paging.

```
A            R SF1CTL                    SFLCTL(SFL1)

A*

A                                        SFLSIZ(0015)

A                                        SFLPAG(0015)

A                                        OVERLAY

A                                        ROLLUP

A                                        ROLLDOWN

A N32                                    SFLDSP

A N31                                    SFLDSPCTL

A  31                                    SFLCLR

A  90                                    SFLEND(*MORE)

A            RRN1          4S 0H         SFLRCDNBR

A                                6  2'Last Name'

A                                        DSPATR(HI)

A                                6 26'First Name'

A                                        DSPATR(HI)

A                                6 50'MI'
```

Continued

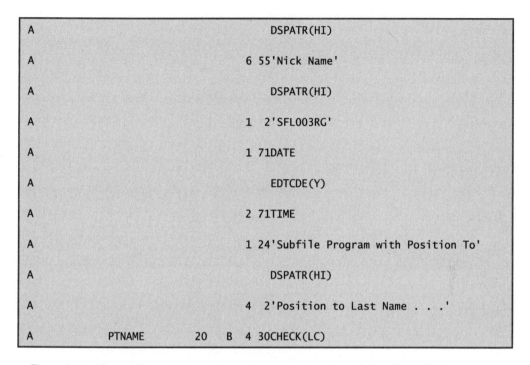

```
A                                    DSPATR(HI)

A                              6 55'Nick Name'

A                                    DSPATR(HI)

A                              1  2'SFL003RG'

A                              1 71DATE

A                                    EDTCDE(Y)

A                              2 71TIME

A                              1 24'Subfile Program with Position To'

A                                    DSPATR(HI)

A                              4  2'Position to Last Name . . .'

A           PTNAME      20   B  4 30CHECK(LC)
```

Figure 2.12: The subfile control record for the page-at-a-time subfile (SFL003DF).

While the RPG program is now a little more complex, it's still not too horribly complicated. In the D specs shown in Figure 2.13, I have added two stand-alone fields,

```
FSfl003df  cf   e            Workstn

F                                    Sfile(Sfl1:Rrn1)

F                                    Infds(Info)

FSfl001lf  if   e        k Disk



DInfo           ds
                                                    Continued
```

```
D Cfkey                      369     369


DSvlnam             S                     Like(Dblnam)

DSvfnam             S                     Like(Dbfnam)


DExit               C                     Const(X'33')

DCancel             C                     Const(X'3C')

DEnter              C                     Const(X'F1')

DRollup             C                     Const(X'F5')

DRolldn             C                     Const(X'F4')

DSflpag             C                     Const(15)

DSflpag_Plus_1      C                     Const(16)

Di                  S               4   0 Inz(0)
```

Figure 2.13: The D specs for page-at-a-time subfiles (SFL003RG).

SVLNAM and SVFNAM. These fields will store the first and last names of the first subfile record. Because these fields make up the key to the database I'm using, I'll use them when the user wants to page up through the data.

The mainline code, shown in Figure 2.14, has also changed. Let's look at the WHEN clause for a moment. When the user presses the Page Up key and the subfile has been displayed (indicator 32 is off), the GOBACK subroutine is executed. This subroutine is used for nothing other than setting the pointer correctly in the data file used for loading the subfile. The first record in the subfile sets lower limits (SETLL) in the data file, SFL001LF. The code then performs a DO loop that will read previous records in the SFL001LF up to one greater than the SFLPAG parameter. If it hits the beginning of the data file before the loop is finished, it sets lower limits with *LOVAL, to position the pointer to the top of the file and get out of the loop. By the time the loop has completed, the data file pointer will either be positioned at the top of the file or at some point in the file, as determined by what is contained in SAVKEY and SFLPAG_ PLUS_1.

After the GOBACK subroutine is executed, the subfile is cleared and a new page is loaded, based on where the code left off in the GOBACK subroutine. The user can now page up or down from anywhere in the subfile, with the only limits being the beginning and end of the data file. This removes the 9,999-record limit, which is helpful in many cases.

During the Build_Subfile routine, when the subfile relative record number (RRN1) equals one, DBLNAM is moved to SVLNAM and DBFNAM to SVFNAM. That sets those fields for later use. You'll also notice the addition of a ROLLDN constant. My program will now handle both paging down and paging up through the subfile. The last D spec you see, which is also new, will be used during the page-up process. The main routine of this program resembles what you've seen before, with the exception of the page-up processing caused by adding the ROLLDN keyword in the DDS.

```
/Free


    // Main Routine


    Exsr Clear_Subfile;      // Execute the subfile clear routine.

    Exsr Build_Subfile;      // Execute the subfile build routine.


    Dou  *Inkc or *Inkl;     // Process until F3 or F12 is pressed.
```

Continued

```
   Write Fkey1;              // Display the function key line.

   Exfmt Sf1ctl;             // Display the subfile.



   Select;                   // Process data entered by the user.


     When (Cfkey = Enter) And (Ptname <> *Blanks);

       Setll (Ptname) Sf1001lf;

       Exsr Clear_Subfile; // Execute the subfile clear routine.

       Exsr Build_Subfile; // Execute the subfile build routine.

       Clear Ptname;       // Clear the position-to field.


     When (Cfkey = Rollup) And (Not *In90);

       Exsr Clear_Subfile; // Execute the clear subfile routine.

       Exsr Build_Subfile; // Execute the subfile build routine.


     When (Cfkey = Rolldn) And (Not *In32);

       Exsr Goback;        // Execute the page back/up routine.

       Exsr Clear_Subfile; // Execute the clear subfile routine.
```

Continued

```
        Exsr Build_Subfile; // Execute the subfile build routine.


   Endsl;



 Enddo;



 *Inlr = *On;
```

Figure 2.14: The mainline routine for the page-at-a-time subfile (SFL003RG).

The code for the build and clear routines is the same as in previous programs, but a new routine has been added for paging back. This code, shown in Figure 2.15, is pretty simple. I first perform the SETLL op code on the data file, SFL001LF, using the first and last names of the first subfile record. (Remember SVLNAM and SVFNAM?) Then, I read backward in the file, using the READP operation for one greater than the subfile page

```
Begsr Goback;


Setll (Svlnam:Svfnam) sfl001lf;


  // Re-position pointer in file for rolling backward. If beginning

  // of file is hit, set the file pointer to first record.


For i = 1 to Sflpag_Plus_1;  // Load subfile with one page of data.
```

Continued

```
   Readp Sfl0011f;

  If %eof;

    Setll (*loval) Sfl0011f;

    Leave;

  Endif;

 Endfor;



 Endsr;

/End-Free
```

Figure 2.15: Paging back in a page-at-a-time subfile (SFL003RG).

size, or until I hit the top of the file. At that point, my data file pointer is either at the top of the file or at the record that occupied the top of the previous subfile page. I then call the Build_Subfile routine to build and display the previous page.

Paging Alternatives

Up to this point, you've learned how to page through the subfile using the paging keys, Page Down (Roll Up), and Page Up (Roll Down). You've probably also noticed that each time you press a page key, you get a whole new page of data. This doesn't have to happen. You have some flexibility when deciding how you page through the data, and which keys to use. Two subfile keywords, SFLENTER and SFLROLVAL, give you this flexibility.

SFLENTER

Use the SFLENTER keyword if you want to press the Enter key to page down through the data. Figure 2.16 shows how to code this keyword. It's used in the subfile control format and performs some pretty cool stuff. With this keyword, the Enter and Page Down keys function in the same way: rolling up through a page of the subfile. That's right—not only don't you lose any capabilities, but you gain the Enter key as another way to page down.

```
A                              SFLENTER(CF10)
```

Figure 2.16: The sflenter keyword in the subfile control format allows you to use the Enter key as the roll-up key.

The required parameter determines which key will be used as Enter for this screen. My example uses CF10, which means the user will now press F10 as the Enter key, to pass control back to the program. All this takes place without any modifications to the RPG program. So, go ahead and give it a shot. If you've come from an S/36 shop where Enter was used to page through data (subfiles don't exist on the S/36), or if you just like the idea of pressing Enter to page through the subfile, SFLENTER might be for you.

SFLROLVAL

You might sometimes want to roll less than one page of data. The SFLROLVAL keyword allows you to do just that. By specifying this field-level keyword in the subfile control format, you let the user tell the system how many records to roll.

Figure 2.17 shows how to code this keyword. The ROLVAL field is defined as input/output, which means the user can key into that field. The user can enter a number less than the value of SFLPAG, press the Page Up or Page Down key, and the subfile will page that number of records. The value used for paging will remain the same until the user changes it. If a number greater than SFLPAG is keyed, the value in SFLPAG is used. If a negative number or zero is entered, an error message will be displayed. SFLROLVAL is ignored for page-at-a-time subfiles (SFLSIZ equals SFLPAG). I suggest you give it a shot with either load-all or self-extending subfiles.

```
A          ROLVAL          4S 0B 6 2  SFLROLVAL
```

Figure 2.17: The sflrolval keyword lets the user determine how many records, less than one page, to roll through.

How to Choose

You now have an understanding of the three subfile types. You've seen the subtle differences in coding and might be wondering when to use which one. That's a good question. There are no rules carved in stone stating when to use each type of subfile, but there are some guidelines you can follow.

The load-all subfile is best used when the number of records in the data file from which you're loading is predictable and small. I say predictable *and* small because just one of those attributes is not good enough for a load-all subfile. You might have a data file with a predictable number of records, but if that number is 10,000, the file isn't a good candidate for a load-all subfile. On the other hand, you might have a data file with a relatively small number of records (50, for example), but if the number is going to increase and you're not sure by how many, you might want to avoid a load-all subfile. A prime candidate for a load-all subfile is a state inquiry program because you should be fairly certain how many records are in the file.

You'll need to determine which files and data criteria are good candidates for load-all processing. Over time, as the data matures, you could get yourself in trouble with load-all subfiles. Think about how long you want users to wait to see the data. Users might not be happy having to wait more than a second or two. You should also be aware of how many times a day the program will be run, and by how many users.

The load-all subfile can be quite efficient and effective if coded properly, but it can impact performance and frustrate users if it's not. When coding a load-all program, set the SFLSIZ to the number of records you expect to be in the file. In the case of the state inquiry, you would set the SFLSIZ somewhere around 50. This is the number of records you expect to load every time the program is run. You wouldn't want to set the SFLSIZ of the state inquiry to 10. The program would still work, and the user would still see all the data, but each time the subfile is forced to self-extend, the new records are not contiguous in memory with the originally loaded records. This will slow the program's processing.

Your best bet is to use the load-all process when you're fairly certain about the amount of data that will be loaded, so you can set your SFLSIZ appropriately. The benefits of the load-all subfile are that it's CPU friendly and very easy to code because IBM i handles so much of the work for you. If you start getting into situations where your load-all subfile is doing a lot of self-extension, or you're adding logic to stop your load-all subfile from loading too much by conditioning the DO loop or the WRITE statement, it might be time to change from a load-all to a self-extending subfile.

When you're not sure of the number of records, you predict data growth, or you know the file has too many records to use a load-all subfile, the self-extending subfile might be your answer. The performance of a self-extending subfile is always consistent because you only load one page at a time. This type of program is a little more CPU-intensive because it goes out to the disk every time new records are loaded to the subfile, and the new records are not in contiguous memory with the previously written records. However, once the records are written, scrolling back and forth through them is performed by the OS, as with a load-all subfile. When I'm not certain about the number of records or the potential growth rate of the data, I use this type of subfile.

If the number of potential records exceeds 9,999, I use the page-at-a-time subfile. By loading one page at a time, you're not limited by the number of records. This type of subfile is the most CPU-intensive because the scrolling is all handled by the program. As a result, each time the user scrolls through the data, the program has to go out to disk to get that data. However, if there are hundreds, thousands, or even millions of potential records in your data file, this type of subfile (with position-to capabilities) is the way to go. I also use page-at-a-time subfiles when I want to add user flexibility to an application. As a programmer, you have more control over the subfile with page-at-a-time processing, and as you'll see in a later chapter, this can be beneficial.

You now have at your disposal a subfile type for every occasion. Whether the data has very few records, many records, potential growth, or certain stagnation, you can rest easy knowing you have a proper subfile for it.

Summary

The following are the important, high-level concepts you should take from this chapter:

- There are three types of subfile programs: load-all, self-extending, and page-at-a-time.
- SFLSIZ must be greater than SFLPAG by at least one when you're using load-all and self-extending subfiles.
- SFLSIZ and SFLPAG must be equal and set to whatever will fit on one page for page-at-a-time subfiles.
- Load-all and self-expanding subfiles have a 9,999-record maximum.
- A page-at-a-time subfile can only hold one page of data. Because of that, you would use this method to display data files with more than 9,999 records.
- The paging of data is completely handled by the IBM i OS in the load-all technique. No programming is necessary.
- Paging down is shared between IBM i and your program in a self-extending subfile. Paging up is still handled by IBM i.
- Your program in a page-at-a-time subfile handles all the paging. You get no help from IBM i.

CHAPTER 3

MODIFYING A SUBFILE (CHANGE IS GOOD)

S ubfiles aren't just for displaying data. They're also extremely useful for modifying the data in your data files. As a matter of fact, some of the most powerful subfile programs you'll write are ones that contain update, add, and delete capabilities.

In this chapter, you'll learn different techniques to modify data files using subfiles. You'll also learn when to use certain techniques and not others.

The first technique allows you to update, add, and delete from a name file, which I'll call "Name Master File Maintenance." This program can be used as a template for any name-type master file, such as a customer, salesperson, or vendor file. This program will introduce you to two new DDS keywords, a new RPG operation code, and a familiar RPG operation with a new use.

SFLNXTCHG, READC, SFLRCDNBR . . . Oh Yeah, CHAIN and UPDATE, Too

The Subfile Next Change (SFLNXTCHG) keyword is used to mark subfile records as changed. There are times when your program will modify the contents or attributes of a subfile record before displaying the subfile back to the user. If you want IBM i to recognize those changes, use SFLNXTCHG. For instance, let's say the user types some information into a subfile record. To determine its validity, your program interrogates the information. If the information is incorrect, you might want to display an error message and highlight the incorrect field (discussed later in this chapter).

Using the SFLNXTCHG keyword, you can mark a subfile record as changed, so that no matter what the user does when the subfile is redisplayed on the screen, the program recognizes the record as changed and attempts to revalidate it. Without SFLNXTCHG, you could still warn the user something is wrong, but if he or she chooses to ignore the incorrect record, your program has no knowledge that it needs to be revalidated.

You do not need the SFLNXTCHG keyword for IBM i to recognize that a user has made a change to a subfile record. The system will mark the subfile record as changed whenever a user changes the data in that record. However, if you want to change data in a subfile record from within your program and mark that record as changed, you need to use SFLNXTCHG in your subfile record format and condition it on an indicator.

The SFLRCDNBR keyword lets IBM i know which page of data to display. If you have a subfile with 10 pages of data, and you want to display record 38 of that subfile, SFLRCDNBR enables you to display the page containing that record. You'll learn more about each of these keywords in the upcoming program.

The last thing I'll introduce at this point that's related to subfiles is the READC operation code. The READC operation reads changed records from a subfile. It reads both records that have been changed by the user and those changed in the program and marked as changed by setting on the indicator-conditioning SFLNXTCHG keyword.

Let me tell you a little story about the first subfile programs I wrote. Early in my career, I was asked to create a subfile to list some data and allow the user to change that data. I wrote a self-extending subfile that allowed the user to change a certain field in the subfile. I had never used SFLNXTCHG or READC before, and I didn't know how they were used. I decided that the only way to know which records were changed was to keep hidden fields in my subfile (type H in DDS, as used in the RRN1 field you've seen before) that matched the display fields.

When I loaded my subfile, I loaded both the display fields and their duplicate hidden fields. When control passed back to my program after the EXFMT operation, I set up a DO loop to start with relative record 1 and CHAIN to the subfile. I then checked to see if the display data had changed from the hidden field data. If it had, I knew that was a changed record and would process it. My DO loop continued incrementing my relative record number and chaining to the subfile to check the data and process any changes. The subfile worked and the users were happy with it, but it didn't process very efficiently. The user would sometimes only make one change, but my program would still check every record. I thought there had to be a better way. Well, there was, and by reading on, you will learn about it.

The DDS for the subfile (SFL1) and subfile control (SF1CTL) record formats in SFL004DF look much like those of a self-extending subfile—because that's what it is. In the code in Figure 3.1, notice that I have no ROLLDN keyword defined in the subfile control record format—IBM i will take care of the rolling down for me. Because SFLSIZ is greater than SFLPAG, the subfile will be allowed to expand if the user wants it to. The paging down will be handled by the OS, except when new records are added to the subfile. In that case, it will be done by the program. (For complete code listings, refer to *http://www.mc-store.com/5104.html*.)

```
A            R SFL1                      SFL

A*

A   74                                   SFLNXTCHG

A            DBIDNM    R        H        REFFLD(PFR/DBIDNM *LIBL/SFL001PF)

A            OPTION          1A  B 10  3VALUES(' ' '2' '4' '5')

A            DBLNAM    R         O 10  7REFFLD(PFR/DBLNAM *LIBL/SFL001PF)

A            DBFNAM    R         O 10 31REFFLD(PFR/DBFNAM *LIBL/SFL001PF)

A            DBMINI    R         O 10 55REFFLD(PFR/DBMINI *LIBL/SFL001PF)

A            DBNNAM    R         O 10 60REFFLD(PFR/DBNNAM *LIBL/SFL001PF)

A          R SF1CTL                      SFLCTL(SFL1)

A*

                                                        Continued
```

```
A                                       CF06

A                                       SFLSIZ(0013)

A                                       SFLPAG(0012)

A                                       ROLLUP

A                                       OVERLAY

A N32                                   SFLDSP

A N31                                   SFLDSPCTL

A  31                                   SFLCLR

A  90                                   SFLEND(*MORE)

A              RRN1          4S 0H      SFLRCDNBR

A                                    9  7'Last Name'

A                                       DSPATR(HI)

A                                    9 31'First Name'

A                                       DSPATR(HI)

A                                    9 55'MI'

A                                       DSPATR(HI)

A                                    9 60'Nick Name'

A                                       DSPATR(HI)

A                                    1  2'SFL004RG'

A                                    1 71DATE
```

Continued

```
A                                        EDTCDE(Y)

A                                        2 71TIME

A                                        1 24'Subfile Program with Update     '

A                                        DSPATR(HI)

A                                        4  2'Position to Last Name . . .'

A             PTNAME         20A  B  4 30CHECK(LC)

A                                        9  2'Opt'

A                                        DSPATR(HI)

A                                        6  2'Type options, press Enter.'

A                                        COLOR(BLU)

A                                        7  4'2=Change'

A                                        COLOR(BLU)

A                                        7 19'4=Delete'

A                                        COLOR(BLU)

A                                        7 34'5=Display'

A                                        COLOR(BLU)
```

Figure 3.1: The subfile control and record formats for the Name Master Maintenance program (SFL004DF).

Notice the SFLNXTCHG and SFLRCDNBR keywords in the code, entered in the subfile record format (SFL). SFLNXTCHG is used in the subfile record format (SFL1) and conditioned with indicator 74. This is the indicator I will manipulate in my RPG program to mark subfile records that have been changed, not by the user, but by my program. User changes are marked automatically by IBM i.

The SFLRCDNBR keyword is used with the relative record number field (RRN1) in the subfile control record (SFLCTL). When you implement SFLRCDNBR, the OS will determine on which page the current relative record number sits and cause your program to display that page. Because I want the user to return to where he or she left off when making a change to a particular subfile record, this will be important.

The other thing you will notice about the DDS is that it now has something other than output or hidden fields defined in the subfile record format. Up to this point, you have seen only output (O type) in the subfile control record format. This program defines a field as "B" for both input and output that allows users to select specific options. Each option corresponds to a specific action to perform in the program. The VALUES keyword tells IBM i the valid options that can be entered. Any other options give a warning error. Now, instead of simply displaying data in the subfile, users have the chance to do something with this data.

Figure 3.2 shows the screen this DDS will produce. Users have a couple of different options from which to choose. As before, they can scroll through the data or establish a position to somewhere else in the subfile. You've already seen how to handle that. If the desired data is on the page a user is looking at, he or she can press 2 to edit that record, 5 to display it, or 4 to delete it.

```
SFL004RG              Subfile Program with Update            1/30/11
                                                            05:07:34

Position to Last Name . . .  _____

Type options, press Enter.
  2=Change        4=Delete        5=Display

Opt  Last Name              First Name        MI    Nick Name
  _    Anthony                Tony              A     Bill
  _    Baker                  Ana               C     Abc
  _    Bilog                  Frances           X     Han Sing
  _    Blade                  Billy             B
  _    Capacino               Tony              K     Knuckles
  _    Fleischer              Jim               R     Jimmy
  _    Gandalf                Norm              A     Sammy
  _    Hezikia                Ezikiel           U     Ezy
  _    Jamison                Antwain           F     Anty
  _    Jim                    Coker             W     Bowling Stud
  _    Joey                   Smite             T     Fingahs
  _    Jonas                  Steve             W     Koolaid
                                                              More...

F3=Exit   F6=Add   F12=Cancel
```

Figure 3.2: An example of the update subfile screen.

This brings me to the last new thing about this DDS, which is the second subfile. Yes, you can code multiple subfiles in a display file. However, as you've already seen in Chapter 1, only 24 of your subfiles can be active at one time, and only 12 can be displayed on a single screen. This second subfile, which is very basic and introduces nothing new, is of the load-all nature. I use it to display a confirmation screen before a user deletes records from the data file. Figure 3.3 shows the DDS code for this second subfile.

```
A           R SFL2                      SFL
A*
A             DBIDNM    R       H       REFFLD(PFR/DBIDNM *LIBL/SFL001PF)
A             DBLNAM    R       O  7   3REFFLD(PFR/DBLNAM *LIBL/SFL001PF)
A             DBFNAM    R       O  7 29REFFLD(PFR/DBFNAM *LIBL/SFL001PF)
A*
A*
A           R SF2CTL                    SFLCTL(SFL2)
A*
A                                       SFLSIZ(0016)
A                                       SFLPAG(0015)
A                                       SFLDSP
A  41                                   SFLCLR
A N41                                   SFLDSPCTL
A N41                                   SFLEND(*MORE)
A                                       OVERLAY
                                                        Continued
```

```
A                RRN2           4S OH

A                              3  3'Press Enter to confirm your choice-

A                                 s for Delete.'

A                                 COLOR(BLU)

A                              4  3'Press F12=Cancel to return to chan-

A                                 ge your choices.'

A                                 COLOR(BLU)

A                              6  3'Last Name'

A                                 DSPATR(HI)

A                              6 29'First Name'

A                                 DSPATR(HI)

A                              1 28'Confirm Delete of Records'

A                                 DSPATR(HI)
```

Figure 3.3: The subfile control and record formats for delete confirmation (SFL004DF).

Now let's move on to the RPG code. Figure 3.4 shows the RPG program F specs that will work with this DDS. Notice that I have defined two subfiles in the F specs for display file SFL004DF. These two subfiles correspond to the two subfiles defined in the DDS.

```
FSfl004df  cf   e           Workstn

F                                   Sfile(Sfl1:Rrn1)

F                                   Sfile(Sfl2:Rrn2)

F                                   Infds(Info)
```

Figure 3.4: The F specs for the display file in the RPG program SFL004RG.

When the user presses the Enter key in the main routine with nothing in the position-to field, the Process_Subfile subroutine is executed. This code snippet is shown in Figure 3.5. The Process_Subfile subroutine then reads the changed subfile records and processes them accordingly.

```
When (Cfkey = Enter) And (Ptname = *Blanks);

  Exsr Process_Subfile;  // Process options taken on the subfile.
```

Figure 3.5: Calling the Process_Subfile subroutine when the user presses Enter with nothing in the position-to field (SFL004RG).

Now let's look at the Process_Subfile subroutine, shown in Figure 3.6. This routine contains a DO loop that reads the changed records in SFL1. When a user enters one of the valid options in the options field, including a blank (which can be done with the spacebar or field-exit key), the READC operation picks that record up and runs it through the select routine.

```
Begsr Process_Subfile;



Exsr Clear_Subfile_2; // Clear the confirmation subfile.



Readc Sfl1;           // Read all changed records in the subfile.

Dow Not %eof;         // Do while there are changed records.



  Select;
```

Figure 3.6: Subroutine Process_Subfile, which processes the user options (SFL004RG).

Depending on which option was selected, the program will execute another subroutine (or, in the case of Option 4, write records to another subfile). Selecting Options 2 and 5 will provide the user a detail screen of data related to that subfile record. In this example, the detail screen will contain the address information of the name listed on the subfile record.

It is important to remember that users can select multiple records for processing. That is, a user can select more than one record to be displayed, changed, or deleted. He or she can also select a mixture of the options to be processed. For example, suppose the user wanted to view subfile records 1, 3, and 5, delete records 9 and 10, and change address information on record 7. He or she would simply type the appropriate option next to each of the appropriate subfile records and press Enter.

The subfile records will be processed in the order in which they exist in the subfile. Because this is a self-extending subfile, the user could page down and select other records for processing without losing what was entered on the previous page or pages. The SFLRCDNBR keyword in the DDS allows me to display the page that contains the last record selected for processing by the user. Once the Enter key is pressed, all the changed records will be processed. If the user were to select options and then position to somewhere else in the subfile using the position-to field, however, everything previously selected would be lost. Selecting Option 5 allows the user to view information from the master record.

Figure 3.7 shows the screen that will be displayed when Option 5 is selected from the subfile list. Figure 3.8 displays the associated code.

```
_SFL004RG                Subfile Program with Update              1/30/11
                                                                 05:11:18

  Customer Number: 0000001

  First Name . . : Kevin

  Last Name. . . : Vandever

  Middle Initial : M

  Nick Name. . . : Subfile Man

  Address Line 1 :

  Address Line 2 :

  Address Line 3 :




  F3=Exit    F12=Cancel
```

Figure 3.7: The screen that displays a record's detail.

```
When Option = Display;  // Option 5 is entered in the subfile opt

  Eval Mode = *Blanks;

  Exfmt Panel2;          // Display the Display Detail screen.

  Option = *Blank;       // Blank out option field.

  Update Sfl1;           // Update the subfile.

  If (Cfkey = Exit) or (Cfkey = Cancel);

    Leave;

Endif;
```

Figure 3.8: The code from the Process_Subfile subroutine that processes a detail request from the user (SFL004RG).

Figure 3.9 shows the screen that will be displayed when the user selects Option 2 (update). At first glance, it looks identical to the one in Figure 3.7, but there is a difference: the upper-left corner shows the word "Update." The other, more significant change is that the user is allowed to change the data fields on the displayed screen. This gives the user the ability to select subfile records and change the detailed information in them.

```
SFL004RG              Subfile Program with Update          1/30/11
Update                                                     05:13:49

   Customer Number . : 0000034

   First Name. . . . . Ezikiel

   Last Name . . . . . Hezikia

   Middle Initial. . . U

   Nick Name . . . . . Ezy

   Address Line 1. . . 13 North St.

   Address Line 2. . . Apt 13

   Address Line 3. . . Berlin, NH 99999




   F3=Exit   F12=Cancel
```

Figure 3.9: The screen that is used to update a record.

Figure 3.10 shows the code for the screen in Figure 3.9.

```
When Option = Change;    // Option 2 is entered in the subfile opt

  Eval Mode = 'Update';

  Exsr Change_Detail;    // Display the Change Detail screen.

  Option = *Blank;       // Blank out option field.

                                                        Continued
```

```
Update Sfl1;              // Update the subfile.

If (Cfkey = Exit) or (Cfkey = Cancel);

   Leave;

Endif;
```

Figure 3.10: The code from Process_Subfile that processes an update request from the user (SFL004RG).

Now let's talk about Option 4, which lets the user delete records from the data file. It's important, as well as courteous, to provide a confirmation screen before allowing the user to delete records from a data file. I do this by building a load-all subfile that contains the records the user has selected for deletion. When the READC loop is finished processing (that is, after all the records selected by the user have been interrogated), I check to see if I loaded any records into the delete confirmation screen, by checking the relative record number (RRN2). If RRN2 is greater than zero, I display the subfile using the EXFMT operation and wait for the user's response. Figure 3.11 shows the delete confirmation subfile, and Figure 3.12 shows the associated code from the Process_Subfile subroutine.

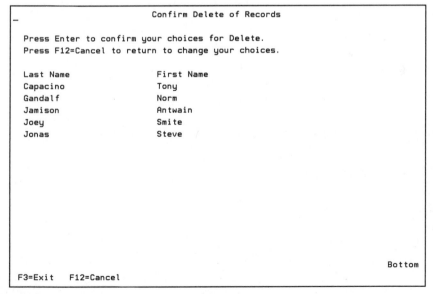

```
_                     Confirm Delete of Records

      Press Enter to confirm your choices for Delete.
      Press F12=Cancel to return to change your choices.

      Last Name                 First Name
      Capacino                  Tony
      Gandalf                   Norm
      Jamison                   Antwain
      Joey                      Smite
      Jonas                     Steve








                                                             Bottom
      F3=Exit    F12=Cancel
```

Figure 3.11: The screen for confirming a delete request.

```
     When Option = Delete;     // Option 4 is entered in the subfile opt

       Rrn2 = Rrn2 + 1;        // Increment the subfile record number.

       Write Sfl2;             // Write the deleted record to subfile.

       *In74 = *On;            // Mark record as changed.

       Update Sfl1;            // Update original subfile as changed.

       *In74 = *Off;           // Reset the SFLNXTCHG indicator.


  Endsl;


    Readc Sfl1;

Enddo;



// If records were selected for delete (4), throw the subfile to

// screen.  If enter is pressed execute the Delete subroutine to

// physically delete the records, clear, and rebuild the subfile

// from the last deleted record (you can certainly position the

// database file where ever you want).


If Rrn2 > 0;

  Lstrrn2 = Rrn2;
```

Continued

```
   Rrn2 = 1;

   Write Fkey2;

   Exfmt Sf2ctl;

   If (Cfkey <> Exit) And (Cfkey <> Cancel);

      Exsr Delete_Record;

      Setll (Dblnam) Sfl001lf;

      Exsr Clear_Subfile_1;

      Exsr Build_Subfile;

   Endif;

Endif;
```

Figure 3.12: The code from Process_Subfile *that processes a delete request from the user (SFL004RG).*

Warning

Remember that the position-to in this self-extending subfile clears and rebuilds the subfile. If you use this example, be careful not to reposition the subfile with the position-to field unless you have processed all of your selections. Of course, you can change the logic to process the selected options before repositioning the subfile, by executing the Process_Subfile subroutine in the position-to When clause of the main routine, but I chose not to do that in this case.

Notice that when I write to the delete confirmation subfile (SFL2) in the Process_Subfile subroutine, I set on indicator 74 to activate the SFLNXTCHG keyword and update SFL1 with the UPDATE keyword. I then deactivate SFLNXTCHG by setting off indicator 74. This marks that subfile record for change, even though it has already been read by the READC operation and the user has made no other changes to that record. This is how I mark a record for change inside my program. Because I didn't clear the options field before updating the subfile, the "4" remains on the subfile record. This way, the user can choose to remove any records he or she doesn't want to delete, press Enter, and the records left marked "magically" show up on the delete confirmation screen.

Figure 3.13 shows the screen displayed if the user selects F12 from the delete confirmation screen. Notice that the records selected for deletion are still marked with 4s. I did this in case the user didn't like what he or she saw on the confirmation screen and wanted to "undelete" an individual entry or two. The user could simply press F12, remove the 4s from the records to "undelete," and then press Enter to get a new confirmation screen, without reentering all the records to be deleted. The SFLNXTCHG keyword makes this possible.

```
SFL004RG              Subfile Program with Update            1/30/11
                                                            05:17:23

   Position to Last Name . . .  _____
                                =

   Type options, press Enter.
     2=Change         4=Delete        5=Display

   Opt   Last Name           First Name         MI   Nick Name
     _   Anthony             Tony               A    Bill
     _   Baker               Ana                C    Abc
     _   Bilog               Frances            X    Han Sing
     _   Blade               Billy              B
     4   Capacino            Tony               K    Knuckles
     _   Fleischer           Jim                R    Jimmy
     4   Gandalf             Norm               A    Sammy
     _   Hezikia             Ezikiel            U    Ezy
     4   Jamison             Antwain            F    Anty
     _   Jim                 Coker              W    Bowling Stud
     4   Joey                Smite              T    Fingahs
     4   Jonas               Steve              W    Koolaid
                                                             More...

    F3=Exit   F6=Add   F12=Cancel
```

Figure 3.13: Redisplaying the original choices when the user cancels from the delete confirmation screen.

Figure 3.14 shows the Delete_Record subroutine, which is executed from the Process_ Subfile subroutine when the user specifies delete. The program clears the original subfile (SFL1) and reloads it—minus the deleted records, of course.

```
Begsr Delete_Record;



For i = 1 to Lstrrn2;    // Loop until no more records to delete.

  Delete (Dbidnm) Pfr;

Endfor;



Endsr;
```

Figure 3.14: The Delete_Record *subroutine deletes the records selected by the user (SFL004RG).*

Add to the Fun with Add Capability

This program also includes the ability to add records to the data file. I won't detail this logic because it really has nothing to do with subfiles. The user can press F6 to add a record to the data file. The program then displays a screen similar to that used for modification (Option 2 from the subfile). The user can enter the new information and add that data to the data file by pressing Enter. Once the add routine is finished, the program clears and reloads the subfile so it will include the newly added record.

You're Now Ready for Master File Maintenance

You've just seen a very useful template for a Name Master File Maintenance program. The user can view, change, and delete data from a data file. I use this type of subfile program when I'm working with files that will have a limited number of additions and modifications.

"What's limited?" you might ask. For me, limited is something of master file-like quality. Master files are not transactional files, meaning you won't have users pounding away at the keyboard adding data to them. My program doesn't lend itself very well to that kind of work. For one, you have to press F6 every time you want to add a record.

This becomes very time consuming if there are hundreds or thousands of records to add to a file, as is sometimes the case with transactional-type files such as an order-entry detail file.

So far, this program is actually kind of boring when it comes to new subfile techniques. Nothing new really happened to the subfile, except that it was used to select records for further processing. Next, you'll learn a subfile technique that's not only able to keep up with the most skilled data-entry professional, but might even enhance his or her skills. This subfile program uses the same capabilities as the previous Name Master File Maintenance program, but in a completely different way, and with the subfile taking a more active role. The display file (SFL005DF) and the RPG program (SFL005RG) for this example are included in their entirety at *http://www.mc-store.com/5104.html*.

SFLINZ, SFLRNA, and Input Subfiles

In the Name Master File Maintenance program, you added records by pressing F6 and filling in a data entry screen. However, depending on the number of fields you're dealing with, you might be able to input data into your data file directly from your subfile records. Implementing input subfiles is a technique that allows for maximum data-entry capabilities. With this type of subfile, you get a page of blank subfile records that you can fill with data, pressing Enter or another valid function key when you're ready to write to a file.

Using this technique, you can build a complete file maintenance program that includes the same update and delete capabilities as the previous example. In addition, you can use it if you have a master-type file with a limited number of fields and want to use a subfile program for maintenance.

The Hard Way

First, let's concentrate on input only. Remember the story of my first subfile program? Well, as part of that project, I had to give the user a separate screen to add new data to the data file. Again, without much subfile knowledge, and not willing to do a little research first, I dug right in. I created a load-all subfile with about 50 records. In the subfile load routine of my RPG program, I cleared the subfile using the SFLCLR keyword, performed a DO loop 50 times, and wrote empty records into the subfile. Just as before, this approach worked, and the users had their 50 records to enter data. I then chained to all 50, looking for non-blank records to write to my data file.

The Correct Way

I've already explained that I should have used READC to read my changed records, but there's more. I could have written the 50 blank records to my subfile without using a DO loop in my RPG, by using the subfile initialize (SFLINZ) keyword in the DDS instead of subfile clear (SFLCLR). SFLINZ works just like SFLCLR, except that instead of creating an empty subfile, SFLINZ provides you with a subfile with the number of records specified in your SFLSIZ keyword. These fields, depending on their types, will all be initialized to zeros or blanks. Figure 3.15 shows the use of the SFLINZ keyword.

```
A                R SF1CTL                      SFLCTL(SFL1)

A                                              SFLSIZ(0050)

A                                              SFLPAG(0017)

A                                              OVERLAY

A N32                                          SFLDSP

A N31                                          SFLDSPCTL

A   31                                         SFLINZ

A                                              SFLRNA

A   90                                         SFLEND(*MORE)

A                RRN1          4S 0H           SFLRCDNBR(CURSOR)
```

Figure 3.15: A subfile control record format with keywords used to initialize a subfile with active and inactive records (SFL005DF).

This subfile is very easy to code. The DDS is as simple as the first load-all subfile from Chapter 1. The RPG is also very simple. There's no load routine to get the initialized records, just a routine to read the changed records using the READC operation and process those changes. A keyword you can use along with the SFLINZ keyword is the subfile record not active (SFLRNA) keyword, also shown in Figure 3.15. This keyword works in conjunction with the SFLINZ keyword to make the initialized records inactive. You might want to make subfile records inactive if you plan to provide a way for the user to add data to a file. You can initialize a page of empty subfile records and make them inactive until the user enters something into the empty subfile record. A subfile can have inactive subfile records. In fact, the only way to make subfile records inactive is by specifying SFLRNA with the SFLINZ keyword.

Let's look at the three ways to make subfile records active:

- When a record is written to the subfile record format using the RPG WRITE operation, that record is active.
- If the user keys data or changes the record of an inactive record (by pressing the spacebar or Field Exit key), that record becomes active.
- Specifying the SFLINZ keyword without the SFLRNA keyword renders the subfile active.

Specifying SFLRNA in my DDS makes my 50 initialized records inactive. Because the READC operation will only look for changes in active records, I will save CPU processing time. If I make changes in only one of my 50 initialized records, the READC operation is going to check only that one record because it's the only active record in the subfile. By using SFLRNA, I can almost get away with not using READC to process my changes. I could simply code a DO loop to start at relative record 1, chain to each subfile record to see if data has been entered, process the data, increment the relative record number, and perform the chain again. This is because the CHAIN command only recognizes active subfile records, just as READC does.

The problem with using CHAIN instead of READC, even with inactive records, is that CHAIN cannot work with a mixture of inactive and active records. For example, if the user enters data on record 1, tabs through record 2, leaving it inactive, and enters data on record 3, the conditional indicator on the CHAIN operation would be set on the first time it hits an inactive record. Logic would therefore pass out of the loop. The second changed record would be skipped because a CHAIN on an inactive record behaves like a no-hit on a database file. READC is smart enough to process all the changed records, even if there are inactive records between them. It's therefore in your best interest to use READC even if you use SFLRNA with SFLINZ. This combination ensures that your program will process all the changed records while reading the minimum amount of subfile records.

Figure 3.16 shows the RPG code that processes the subfile. Except for having to clear the subfile first, it looks just like the previous program.

```
Begsr Process_Subfile;



Readc Sfl1;              // Read all changed records in the subfile.

Dow Not %eof;            // Do while there are changed records.



  Select;



    When In_lnam > *blanks;      // Only process non blank last name

      Setgt (*Hival) Sfl001pf;

      Readp Sfl001pf;            // Retrieve the highest ID number.

      In_dbidnm = Dbidnm;        // Save the number in a save field.

      Clear Pfr;                 // Clear the database record

      Dbidnm = In_dbidnm + 1;    // New ID number for added record.

      Dblnam = In_lnam;          // Move screen data to database.

      Dbfnam = In_fnam;
```

Continued

```
        Dbmini = In_mini;

        Dbnnam = In_nnam;

        Write Pfr;                    // Write new database record.




    Ends1;



Readc Sfl1;

Enddo;


Endsr;
```

Figure 3.16: Processing a subfile with READC when SFLRNA and SFLINZ have been specified in the DDS (SFL005RG).

SFLCSRPRG and Input Subfiles

Use of the subfile cursor progression (SFLCSRPRG) keyword can also help the data-entry professional. I use this field when I want to control which field the cursor goes to when the Tab or Field Exit key is pressed. The normal progression of the cursor is from left to right across the screen, moving to all input-capable fields on one line before going to the first field on line 2.

Let's say the normal progression is not how the user wants to enter the data. Maybe the user wants to enter all the last names first, and then the first names. SFLCSRPRG lets you accomplish this. You just place the SFLCSRPRG keyword under the field where you want the cursor to progress, and away you go. Figure 3.17 shows an example.

```
A            R SFL1                    SFL

A*

A              IN_LNAM   R        B   5  2REFFLD(PFR/DBLNAM *LIBL/SFL001PF)

A                                        SFLCSRPRG

A                                        CHECK(LC)

A              IN_FNAM   R        B   5 26REFFLD(PFR/DBFNAM *LIBL/SFL001PF)

A                                        CHECK(LC)

A              IN_MINI   R        B   5 50REFFLD(PFR/DBMINI *LIBL/SFL001PF)

A                                        CHECK(LC)

A              IN_NNAM   R        B   5 55REFFLD(PFR/DBNNAM *LIBL/SFL001PF)

A                                        CHECK(LC)
```

Figure 3.17: This code allows the user to fill in the last name of all the subfile records before moving to the next field (SFL005DF).

The keyword isn't activated until the cursor enters the field on which you defined SFLCSRPRG. Because the last name is the first entry field in my program, the cursor would start out on first name, and the user, using Tab or Field Exit, could either enter the first name or move to the last name. Once there, the user would enter a last name and press Tab or Field Exit. The cursor would jump down to the next record in the last-name field. Using this technique, the user could enter all the last names before entering any first names, without having to use any extra keystrokes. Entering names of people might not be the best application of this technique, but you can probably think of other examples where it would come in handy.

If you had more fields in the subfile but wanted to fill each column first before moving on to the next field, you could place SFLCSRPRG on every field in the subfile. This would cause your cursor to move top to bottom instead of left to right for all fields. One potential problem with this is that SFLCSRPRG will only work with device controllers that can handle the enhanced data stream. If you run into problems using this keyword, your controller might not be able to handle the enhanced data stream.

SFLINZ, SFLRNA, SFLRCDNBR, and Update Subfiles

As cool as input subfiles are, an application alone they do not make. Let's look back to the original Name Master File Maintenance program for a minute. Why couldn't you use this type of subfile technique with the Name Master file? Why should you have to press F6 every time you want to add a record? You've seen that you don't always have to use a function key to add records. You can now add records directly from my subfile.

What about update and delete? Instead of Option 2 to update the data or Option 4 to delete a record, why can't you just type over, or blank out, the data in the subfile, and update the file that way? The truth is that you can use this type of program for master file maintenance.

The program we'll discuss next is another version of the Name Master File Maintenance program, and also an extension of our input subfile program. Figure 3.18 shows what the new maintenance screen will look like.

```
SFL005RG            Add Data to Blank Subfile Lines              1/30/11
                                                                05:19:53


  Last Name              First Name        MI    Nick Name
  Kent                   Craig             S     Craig
  Laut                   Kim               O     Kimmy
  Mustard                Mitchell          A     Mitch
  Patterson              Tony              C     T
  Smith                  Tim               X     Smitty
  Suanzie                Lesile            Q     Leapin' Lesile
  Tarrney                Modesto           T     Mo
  Train                  Bob               W     Chowdah
  Vandever               Corina            R     Wine Diva
  Vandever               Felicia           R     Fish
  Vandever               Kalia             M     Smiley
  Vandever               Kevin             M     Subfile Man
  _____                _____        _     _____
  _____                _____        _     _____
  _____                _____        _     _____
  _____                _____        _     _____
  _____                _____        _     _____
                                                           More...

  F3=Exit    F12=Cancel
```

Figure 3.18: An alternative update/add subfile technique (SFL007RG).

This program provides the user with a load-all subfile that allows all the data fields to be changed. There are no options to be taken to display, change, or delete the data. To add records, you simply page to the end of the subfile and enter data in the empty subfile records. There is no F6 key to press. To change data records, you simply type over the data in the subfile record, and the data will be updated in the data file the next time Enter is pressed. To delete records, you press Field Exit through the data fields of a subfile record to make them blank, and that record will be deleted from the data file. The complete code for this program is at *http://www.mc-store.com/5104.html*.

Tying It All Together

Let's look first at the DDS, shown in Figure 3.19. Notice that I define all my fields as type B, just as I did in the input subfile. Remember, the "B" means input/output. I have also added a hidden field to hold the identification number. The hidden field is the key to the physical file that I'll use to delete records. If the user blanks out a subfile record, I can still preserve the key data to the file in the hidden field. My program can then CHAIN to the physical file using the hidden field and delete that record from the file. In addition to hidden fields being used to preserve data on input/output subfile records, as you've just seen, they are also valuable when you want to maintain some information about a specific subfile record, but don't want to display that data on the screen.

```
A           DBIDNM    R       H       REFFLD(PFR/DBIDNM *LIBL/SFL001PF)

A           DBLNAM    R       B   5  2REFFLD(PFR/DBLNAM *LIBL/SFL001PF)

A                                     CHECK(LC)

A           DBFNAM    R       B   5 26REFFLD(PFR/DBFNAM *LIBL/SFL001PF)

A                                     CHECK(LC)

A           DBMINI    R       B   5 50REFFLD(PFR/DBMINI *LIBL/SFL001PF)

A                                     CHECK(LC)

A           DBNNAM    R       B   5 55REFFLD(PFR/DBNNAM *LIBL/SFL001PF)

A                                     CHECK(LC)
```

Figure 3.19: A load-all subfile with input/output-capable fields.

Because I want blank lines to follow the current data in the file, this will be a load-all subfile program. Because I'm going to allow entry fields for adding data, I'm going to use SFLINZ instead of SFLCLR. Assuming that I've made SFLSIZ large enough, this will give me the desired lines at the end of my subfile. To offset making SFLSIZ too large, I'll use SFLRNA to make the blank subfile records inactive. They'll only be made active, and therefore dealt with by the CPU, by one of the three ways mentioned earlier in this chapter.

Now for the RPG. I turn on indicator 31 to initialize 50 inactive records and load all the data from my data file. Because the records are inactive, I can use the WRITE operation to load data into them. If the subfile records were active, I would have to CHAIN to the subfile and UPDATE it with the information from the data file.

Normally, you use the WRITE operation to write records to the subfile. If you had initialized 50 records, as I did, and made them active, you would have to CHAIN to the active, but empty, subfile record, and UPDATE it with the data. Because I initialized the subfile and made the records inactive (SFLRNA), I'm still able to use the WRITE operation to get data into the subfile. Got it? (Sorry—I just want to make sure you understand the difference.) Figure 3.20 shows this segment of the code.

```
Begsr Build_Subfile;


*In31 = *on;          // Turn on subfile initialize.

Rrn1 = 1;

Write Sflctl;         // Write blank records to the screen.

Rrn1 = 0;             // Reset to 0 for subfile build.

*In31 = *off;

                                              Continued
```

```
Setll (*Loval) Sfl0011f;

Read Sfl0011f;



Dow (Not %eof) And (Rrn1 <= 50);  // Process up to 50 records.

  Dbidnm = In_dbidnm;

  Dblnam = In_dblnam;

  Dbfnam = In_dbfnam;

  Dbmini = In_dbmini;

  Dbnnam = In_dbnnam;

  Rrn1 = Rrn1 + 1;

  Write Sfl1;

  Read Sfl0011f;

Enddo;
```

Figure 3.20: Loading data into the subfile (SFL007RG).

Once I'm finished loading the subfile and allowing it to be displayed by setting the appropriate indicator, I display it to the user. Paging down through the subfile, the user eventually comes to the end of the data and the beginning of the blank lines. To modify a record, he or she simply keys over the data in the subfile record. To delete a record, he or she blanks out the data on the subfile record. (I've made it so the user only has to blank out the last name.) To add a record, he or she keys data into one of the blank lines.

Once the Enter key is pressed, the program processes the changed records in the Process_Subfile subroutine, using a READC loop, the hidden field, and the data entered in the subfile to analyze what to do with the record. If the subfile (or last name, in this case) is empty but there's something in the hidden field, that record is a candidate for deletion because it holds the hidden key. If there's data in the subfile but nothing in the hidden field, that's an add. If READC detects a changed record with data in the record and something in the hidden field, that record is a modification to an existing record. Figure 3.21 shows the Process_Subfile subroutine that does all of this fine work. Notice that there's a little more to this version than to the input-subfile version.

```
Begsr Process_Subfile;


Readc Sfl1;              // Read all changed records in the subfile.

Dow Not %eof;           // Do while there are changed records.


  Select;


// Add when hidden field is empty but something's in the subfile



    When (Dbidnm = 0) And (Dblnam > *Blanks);

      Setgt (*Hival) Sfl001pf;

      Readp Sfl001pf;            // Retrieve the highest ID number.

      Up_dblnam = Dblnam;

      Up_dbfnam = Dbfnam;
```

Continued

```
         Up_dbmini = Dbmini;

         Up_dbnnam = Dbnnam;

         Up_dbidnm = Up_dbidnm + 1;

         Write Up_pfr;


// Update when hidden field is not empty and neither is last name


      When (Dbidnm <> 0) And (Dblnam > *Blanks);

         Chain Dbidnm Sfl001pf;

         If %found;

           Up_dblnam = Dblnam;

           Up_dbfnam = Dbfnam;

           Up_dbmini = Dbmini;

           Up_dbnnam = Dbnnam;

           Update Up_pfr;

         Endif;


// Delete when hidden field is not empty but last name is empty


      When (Dbidnm <> 0) And (Dblnam = *Blanks);
```

Continued

```
    Chain Dbidnm Sf1001pf;

    If %found;

      Delete Up_pfr;

    Endif;



  Ends1;



Readc Sfl1;

Enddo;



Endsr;
```

Figure 3.21: This routine processes all the options selected by the user.

More on Update

I'm not validating any information on the subfile records. I'm simply allowing the user to key data, and then I'm doing something with that data. Now I want to change my program so that the user is not allowed to add data if the last-name field is blank. I will show you how to modify a subfile record's attributes, in addition to modifying the contents of the subfile. Figure 3.22 shows the DDS source to add.

```
A                DBLNAM    R            B 5   2REFFLD(PFR/DBLNAM *LIBL/SFL001PF)

A                                             SFLCSRPRG

A                                             CHECK(LC)

A    42                                       DSPATR(RI)

A    42                                       DSPATR(PC)
```

Figure 3.22: Display attributes for the last-name field.

I added two display attribute (DSPATR) keywords, both of which are conditioned on indicator 42. The first DSPATR line says that when indicator 42 is on, set the last name, DBLNAM, to reverse image (RI). The second DSPATR says to position the cursor (PC) to this field when indicator 42 is on. Don't forget to add the SFLNXTCHG keyword and make it active on indicator 74, as you learned earlier in this chapter.

Now let's look at the RPG program, to see how to set those attributes. Figure 3.23 shows the new WHEN clause to handle that. I'm going to reverse-image and position the cursor to any record the READC operation picked up as changed, but in which no last name was entered. This probably means the user keyed some information into the subfile record, but forgot to key the last name. So, I check to see if the last name is blank using a WHEN clause within the READC DO loop. If it's blank, I set on indicator 42, which is the indicator used to condition the DSPATR keywords in my subfile record format, and indicator 74, which is the SFLNXTCHG indicator. I then UPDATE the subfile record.

```
When (Dblnam = *Blanks);

   *In42 = *on;
   *In74 = *on;

   Udate Sfl1;

   *In42 = *off;
   *In74 = *off;
```

Figure 3.23: The logic to change the attributes of a subfile record.

Because indicators 42 and 74 are on, any keywords conditioned within the subfile record format with those indicators will take effect. I then set the indicators off for the next READC iteration. Now when the subfile is displayed, the incorrect (blank last name) field will be displayed in reverse image so it's noticeable to the user, and the cursor will be positioned in that field so the user can easily change the data. If more than one record is in error, the cursor will position to the first record in error, but all the fields in error will display in reverse image.

I set the SFLNXTCHG indicator (74) just in case the user ignores the incorrect data. If that happens, READC will still pick up the field as changed, regardless of what the user does, the next time the subfile is processed. The WHEN clause in Figure 3.23 will be run again, and the field will again be displayed in error.

Another Option

If you feel—or have been told by the user—that this program will be used more to add records than to modify or delete them, you'll want a fast method to get to the first empty record in the subfile. The best way to do that is to use the SFLRCDNBR keyword as before, but with a slight twist. As you might remember, the SFLRCDNBR keyword is used to display the page of the current relative record number. If the relative record number is 16 and record 16 is on the second page of the subfile, the second page will be displayed when the EXFMT operation is used in your program.

The twist to accomplishing this is to add the parameter (CURSOR) to the SFLRCDFMT keyword, as shown in the DDS in Figure 3.24. This displays the page where the current relative record number exists and places the cursor on the exact line that matches the relative record number. Suppose, in your load-all routine, you add one to your relative record number. Instead of initializing it to one after all the data has been loaded from the data file, the program will display the first page with empty subfile records and place the cursor at the first empty subfile line.

```
A              R SF1CTL                        SFLCTL(SFL1)

A*

A                                              SFLSIZ(0050)

A                                              SFLPAG(0017)

A                                              OVERLAY

A N32                                          SFLDSP

A N31                                          SFLDSPCTL

A   31                                         SFLINZ

A                                              SFLRNA

A   90                                         SFLEND(*MORE)

A              RRN1           4S 0H            SFLRCDNBR(CURSOR)
```

Figure 3.24: Using SFLRCDNBR(CURSOR) to display the first page of empty subfile records.

Look Before You Leap

Before using this technique to modify or delete records from a data file, there are a couple of things you need to take into consideration. First, when deleting records this way, you're providing no confirmation to the user. A record could be inadvertently cleared and subsequently deleted, without the user ever knowing it. Also, updating and record-locking become a bit more crucial using this technique. Each time a record is displayed for update in the first maintenance program, it's retrieved from the data file. The record is easily locked while the user remains on the update screen.

The number of records in the data file should also be taken into consideration, as this application employs a load-all subfile. In Chapter 2 where you first learned about that kind of subfile, I discussed when it should and should not be used.

In the third example (the input subfile being the second), all the data is loaded at the beginning of the program. You can change any record as you scroll through the data. However, the data might have changed between the time it was added to the subfile, when it is finally modified in the subfile, and when you press Enter to update the data file. If other users are able to get into this program at the same time, they might not have the most current changes. They might also make changes, thus wiping out the other changes. You can certainly allocate the files to one use of the program and solve the problem. The fact remains, though, that data integrity must be considered along with the speed of entry when you design a file-maintenance subfile program.

Summary

The following are the important, high-level concepts and new keywords you should take from this chapter:

- Use the CHAIN operation to access a subfile record by relative record number.
- Use UPDATE to update a specific subfile record after a CHAIN or READC has accessed that record.
- READC reads only changed records in your subfile.
- SFLNXTCHG allows you to mark records as changed in your program, without user intervention, so the READC operation will pick them up.
- SFLRCDNBR allows you to display a specific page of a subfile based on the relative record number.
- SFLINZ allows you to create a subfile full of initialized records, eliminating the need for a DO loop in your RPG program to accomplish this task.
- SFLRNA works in conjunction with SFLINZ to make the initialized records inactive and save processing time.
- SFLCSRPGR allows you to change the way data is entered on the subfile. Instead of left-to-right data entry, you might want to allow top-to-bottom entry. This keyword only works if the device controller can handle the enhanced data stream.
- Using a full-fledged input and update subfile requires some thought about data integrity versus speed of entry. Make sure you engage in the analysis stage before using this kind of subfile for master file maintenance.

CHAPTER 4

WINDOW SUBFILES: WHO NEEDS A PC TO HAVE SCROLLABLE WINDOWS?

This chapter discusses windows and windowed subfiles. To show you how easy windowed subfiles are to implement, let's revisit the Name Master File Maintenance program from the previous chapter. Remember the delete-confirmation screen, which listed the subfile records selected for deletion by the user? Figure 4.1 shows it.

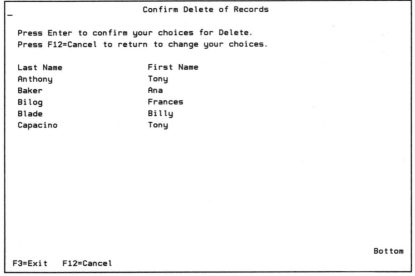

```
                         Confirm Delete of Records
  _
     Press Enter to confirm your choices for Delete.
     Press F12=Cancel to return to change your choices.

     Last Name              First Name
     Anthony                Tony
     Baker                  Ana
     Bilog                  Frances
     Blade                  Billy
     Capacino               Tony




                                                              Bottom
     F3=Exit    F12=Cancel
```

Figure 4.1: The original design of the delete-confirmation screen.

What if you want to see part of the data from the original screen while you're looking at the confirmation screen? Or maybe you want to see whether there are records from the original subfile to delete, without having to press F12 from the confirmation screen. Figure 4.2 shows the confirmation screen redesigned as a windowed subfile. The transformation was extremely easy to create and required very few changes to the RPG program.

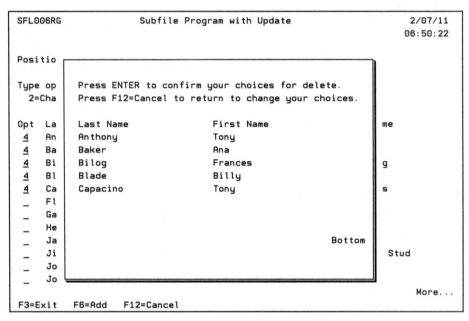

Figure 4.2: The delete-confirmation screen as a window.

So Little Changed, So Much Accomplished

Figure 4.3 shows the DDS for the new windowed subfile. Note that I changed the record format name from SFL1 to WINDOW1. I didn't have to, but I think this better reflects that it's a windowed subfile. Because it's still in the subfile record format, I give it the SFL keyword.

```
A          R WINDOW1                    SFL
A*
A           DBIDNM    R        H       REFFLD(PFR/DBIDNM *LIBL/SFLOO1PF)
A           DBLNAM    R        O  6   2REFFLD(PFR/DBLNAM *LIBL/SFLOO1PF)
A           DBFNAM    R        O  6  26REFFLD(PFR/DBFNAM *LIBL/SFLOO1PF)
A*
A          R SF2CTL                     SFLCTL(WINDOW1)
A*
A                                       SFLDSP
A N41                                   SFLDSPCTL
A  41                                   SFLCLR
A N41                                   SFLEND(*MORE)
A                                       SFLSIZ(0009)
A                                       SFLPAG(0008)
A                                       WINDOW(4 10 16 52)
A           RRN2           4S OH
A                                     5  2'Last Name'
A                                       DSPATR(HI)
A                                     5 26'First Name'
A                                       DSPATR(HI)
```

Continued

```
A                                    2  2'Press ENTER to confirm your choice-

A                                       s for delete.'

A                                       COLOR(BLU)

A                                    3  2'Press F12=Cancel to return to chan-

A                                       ge your choices.'

A                                       COLOR(BLU)
```

Figure 4.3: The DDS for a windowed subfile (SFL006DF).

I occasionally use Screen Design Aid (SDA) to code display formats. It's interesting to note that, when you select Option 1 to add a new format, SDA will prompt you to provide the type of record format. Instead of selecting SFL as you would with a normal subfile record format, you would select Window Subfile (WDWSFL). SDA will then prompt you for the subfile control record format that controls this subfile, and you'll enter the name as normal. (I still used SF2CTL in my example.)

This is important because if you're using SDA and enter WDWSFL as the type of record format, SDA will provide you with both the subfile and the window keywords to use. Selecting type SFL in SDA won't provide you the opportunity to define window keywords. You'll have to do so directly in the code. Also, even though you define the record format as WDWSFL, it will show up as SFL in your DDS specifications. I bring this up because many programmers use SDA, so it can be beneficial to know how SDA works with subfiles and windows, especially as it relates to the WDWSFL-to-SFL keyword quirk.

The other change you'll notice in the subfile record format is that the starting positions are different. The new starting positions are related to the window, not the entire screen. Regardless of where you position your window, the starting points for the fields will be in column 2 of that window. This allows you to display the window based on the cursor position, as well as the hard-coded starting positions.

In the subfile control record format, notice that only two things have changed. First, I added the WINDOW keyword. The WINDOW keyword describes the length, width, and position of the window. In my example, the window starts in row 4, column 10, and is 16 lines long and 52 characters wide. The second change is to the OVERLAY keyword, which allows me to overlay the previous data without clearing the screen. That's it for the DDS.

All I had to do in the RPG program was change the name of the subfile record format. Instead of writing to SFL1, I now write to WINDOW1. Now, when you select records to be deleted, you will see the new windowed subfile as the confirmation screen.

Figure 4.4 shows the changed RPG code in the F specification: the definition of WINDOW1 instead of SFL2.

```
FSf1006df  cf   e              Workstn

F                              Sfile(Sfl1:Rrn1)

F                              Sfile(Window1:Rrn2)

F                              Infds(Info)
```

Figure 4.4: Modifications to the F specification to use the new windowed subfile (SFLO06RG).

The Process_Subfile subroutine in Figure 4.5 will read the changed records from SFL1 and process those entries. If there are records selected for deletion, the routine will write to, and read from, WINDOW1 to process the deleted records. The complete source is available at *http://www.mc-store.com/5104.html*.

```
Begsr Process_Subfile;



Exsr Clear_Subfile_2; // Clear the confirmation subfile.



Readc Sfl1;           // Read all changed records in the subfile.

                                                          Continued
```

```
Dow Not %eof;          // Do while there are changed records.



  Select;



    When Option = Display;  // Option 5 is entered in the subfile opt

      Eval Mode = *Blanks;

      Exfmt Panel2;        // Display the Display Detail screen.

      Option = *Blank;     // Blank out option field.

      Update Sfl1;         // Update the subfile.

      If (Cfkey = Exit) or (Cfkey = Cancel);

        Leave;

      Endif;



    When Option = Change;   // Option 2 is entered in the subfile opt

      Eval Mode = 'Update';

      Exsr Change_Detail;   // Display the Change Detail screen.

      Option = *Blank;      // Blank out option field.

      Update Sfl1;          // Update the subfile.

      If (Cfkey = Exit) or (Cfkey = Cancel);
```

Continued

```
      Leave;

    Endif;



    When Option = Delete;     // Option 4 is entered in the subfile opt

      Rrn2 = Rrn2 + 1;        // Increment the subfile record number.

      Write Window1;          // Write the deleted record to subfile.

      *In74 = *On;            // Mark record as changed.

      Update Sfl1;            // Update original subfile as changed.

      *In74 = *Off;           // Reset the SFLNXTCHG indicator.



  Endsl;



  Readc Sfl1;

Enddo;



// If records were selected for delete (4), throw the subfile to

// screen.  If enter is pressed execute the Delete subroutine to

// physically delete the records, clear, and rebuild the subfile

// from the last deleted record (you can certainly position the
```

Continued

```
// database file where ever you want).


If Rrn2 > 0;

  Lstrrn2 = Rrn2;

  Rrn2 = 1;

  Exfmt Sf2ctl;

  If (Cfkey <> Exit) And (Cfkey <> Cancel);

    Exsr Delete_Record;

    Setll (Dblnam) Sfl001lf;

    Exsr Clear_Subfile_1;

    Exsr Build_Subfile;

  Endif;

Endif;


Endsr;
```

Figure 4.5: The subroutine to process the subfile entries.

You've just seen an extremely simple example of a windowed subfile. Really, it's pretty simple to implement a windowed subfile, no matter how you do it, because

IBM i does so much of the work for you. The RPG has barely changed from the Name Master File Maintenance program in the last chapter. You can see here the power of DDS to control the display features of a screen. RPG is only along for the ride.

SFLEND and the Bar Scene

To add a little pizzazz to the screen, you can add a scroll bar to either or both of the subfiles in this program. Let's add a scroll bar to the confirmation window from the previous example, as shown in Figure 4.6.

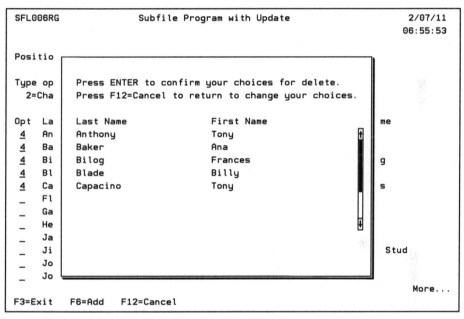

Figure 4.6: A windowed subfile with a scroll bar.

In the discussion of the SFLEND keyword in Chapter 1, I mentioned that it had other valid parameters that would be discussed later. Well, it's later. In the subfile control record format, SF2CTL, I'll change the SFLEND keyword parameter from *MORE to *SCRBAR, recompile my DDS and program, and—voilà! Notice, in Figure 4.7, that the only change is the addition of *SCRBAR to the SFLEND keyword.

```
A           R SF2CTL                      SFLCTL(WINDOW1)

A*

A                                         SFLDSP

A N41                                     SFLDSPCTL

A  41                                     SFLCLR

A N41                                     SFLEND(*SCRBAR *MORE)

A                                         SFLSIZ(0009)

A                                         SFLPAG(0008)

A                                         WINDOW(4 10 16 52)

A           RRN2          4S 0H

A                                5  2'Last Name'

A                                         DSPATR(HI)

A                                5 26'First Name'

A                                         DSPATR(HI)

A                                2  2'Press ENTER to confirm your choice-

A                                         s for delete.'
```
Continued

```
A                                    COLOR(BLU)

A                              3  2'Press F12=Cancel to return to chan-

A                                 ge your choices.'

A                                    COLOR(BLU)
```

Figure 4.7: The SFL record format with coding for a scroll bar (SFL006DF with SFLEND modification).

This scroll bar can be used like a scroll bar on a PC; that is, it can be controlled with a pointing device such as a mouse. It doesn't remove the capability to scroll using the keyboard, but merely provides another option to the user. It's extremely easy to implement. No additional programming had to be done to display and control the scroll bar, and the RPG didn't change at all.

Because not all workstation controllers support pointer devices and scroll bars, you might want to add both the *SCRBAR and *MORE parameters to the SFLEND keyword. That way, if the scroll bar isn't supported, the user will still see "More" and "Bottom" on the lower right of the subfile, as usual. No additional programming had to be done to display and control the scroll bar, and the RPG didn't change at all.

The RPG programs SFL005RG, SFL006RG, and SFL007RG at *http://www.mc-store. com/5104.html* are all basically the same. There are three separate programs simply because I created a new display file with each new feature and changed a record format name or two. As a result, I created separate RPG source members to reflect each change.

But Wait! There's More

You've already seen a few techniques related to windowed subfiles, but I haven't really explained all there is to know about how to implement them. There's more to a windowed subfile than the WINDOW keyword and a new parameter in the SFLEND keyword. Before we go on, I'll define some terms and introduce some new DDS keywords related to windows.

Windows 101

Windows are very powerful tools for displaying subfiles because they do more than just present information in a smaller format. They provide system-resource save and restore functions, cursor control, and message handling, all without much effort by the programmer. With a couple of keyword entries, IBM i will handle much of the work for you.

A window is an area of information that overlays part of your display screen. You may view and update information in the window, as well as view information on the portion of the screen the window isn't covering. When a window is displayed, it's the only part of the screen that's active. As a result, you can't do anything with the screen that the window is covering until the window is removed. You can display up to 12 windows at a time, but no matter how many are displayed, only one can be active at a time.

The *window definition record* is the record format that contains the WINDOW keyword. In the case of my program example, it's the subfile control record format, SF2CTL, for the confirmation screen. You can also have a *window reference* record format. While the window reference format contains the WINDOW keyword, the keyword refers to another format for the actual window attributes. I didn't use it in my example, but it comes in handy when you have multiple windows that all have the same attributes. You can define the attributes in one record format and refer to that format using the WINDOW keyword with the format name as a parameter.

The window border is the area that surrounds the window. In my example, I used the defaults, which means I didn't have to explicitly define them in my DDS. The border doesn't have to be visible. The active window is the one that has had the last input or output operation performed against it. When you use visible borders, the active window will appear to be on top.

When writing multiple window applications, be aware that removing a window from the display and overlaying a window are two different actions. When a window is removed from a display, it's no longer accessible to the user. When a window is overlaid by another, it is inactive and might not be visible, but it is still accessible and can be made active again when the overlaying window is removed.

The Keywords

You have five DDS keywords at your disposal to create windows and window subfiles:

- **WINDOW**—The Window keyword is required to define a window in your application. It's used to define the window, change its contents, or make an inactive window active again. You can define how the program acts when the cursor is outside the window borders, tell where messages are to be displayed, or simply point to another record format to get your attributes.
- **WDWBORDER**—The Window Border keyword defines the color, display attributes, and characters of a window border.
- **WDWTITLE**—The Window Title keyword embeds the title of the window inside the border. Embedded in the top or bottom of the border, it allows you to define the text, color, and attributes for the title of the window. Note, though, that not all workstation controllers support text in the bottom of the border. Note, also, that some do not allow left and right justification of title text.
- **RMVWDW**—The Remove Window keyword removes previous windows when a new window is displayed, or when an existing window is made active by redisplaying.
- **USRRSTDSP**—The User Restore Display keyword stops IBM i from performing automatic save and restore functions on the underlying display when windows are displayed and removed. In most cases, you probably want to allow IBM i to do its thing because it requires no effort on your part. When performance is more of an issue, however, you might want to disable this activity. Preventing the automatic save and restore of the underlying display might improve your response time. You can also use the USRRSTDSP keyword to make an overlaid window pop up and become active, or to make two windows seem like they're both active—something you'll see in Chapter 6.

With these keywords, you make IBM i do a lot for you to create effective and efficient window applications.

Windows 201

In a windowed application, the OS automatically performs save and restore operations. Before a window is displayed, IBM i saves the whole display, including any windows not being removed. When windows are removed, it restores the display, minus the removed windows. If a new window is added to the display, the active record is saved when the new window record is written, and the entire display remains as background data. The new window becomes the active record. The saved record doesn't have to be a window. The OS handles non-window records in the same way if the display files are created (CRTDSPF) with the restore display parameter (RSTDSP) set to *YES.

If the window record being written to the display is a previously existing window, more recent windows are removed without being saved. The target window is then restored by IBM i, the new record is written, and that window becomes active.

If a non-window record is written to the display, all bets are off. Any existing windows are removed without being saved, the new record is written to the display as it existed prior to any windows, and that display becomes active.

IBM i provides these services without any work from you, the programmer. It's best if you know the rules, but you don't really have to. You don't have to think about what's going on beneath the application code. You know IBM i is taking care of you as you display and remove your windows. There are times, however, when you might want to bypass some of the processing provided by IBM i.

Most of the time, this decision will be based on whether your windows are displayed over communication lines or locally. Response time is critical when your users are attached remotely. The save and restore operations performed by IBM i can adversely affect response times for remote users, depending on your communication rate. High-speed communication lines and local area networks (LANs) provide almost local-like responses, and therefore probably need no tweaking. Anything less, such as dialup, might require you to perform some tweaking to improve response times.

More on USRRSTDSP and Tweaking

The USRRSTDSP keyword contains a lot of power. You can use it to bypass the system save and restore processing performed by IBM i and, instead, program your application to rebuild the display only when necessary. This technique can improve system performance and reduce response times for your users. They will love you for it.

As mentioned earlier, you can also have some fun with USRRSTDSP when you want more than one window to seem active at a time. Here are the times when two saves are performed on the same display:

- When your application displays only one window at a time
- When your display file is created with the Restore Display parameter turned on, RSTDSP(*YES)
- When the first window record to overlay the display is located in a separate file

The first save operation is performed when the display file is suspended. The second save operation is performed because a window is being displayed. USRRSTDSP eliminates the second, unnecessary save.

What does IBM say? The following excerpt from *Application Display Programming V5* (SC41-5715, pp. 127–128) explains it well:

> To bypass system save and restore processing, IBM suggests that you perform the following steps:
>
> - Create your own procedure to rebuild the display after a window is removed. Be sure to include any data that the user enters and that must be redisplayed.
> - Specify the record-level USRRSTDSP keyword on the window following the first window you don't want the system to save. The USRRSTDSP keyword keeps the system from performing save and restore operations. The USRRSTDSP keyword is allowed only on records containing the WINDOW keyword; it's ignored on the window reference record.
>
> Once the USRRSTDSP keyword is specified, it remains in effect, even if the option indicator is set off, until you read or write to either the initial, windowless display

or the window that is two windows before the window on which the USRRSTDSP keyword was specified. Assume that six windows are on the display and the USRRSTDSP keyword was specified on the fourth. To turn off USRRSTDSP and have the system resume saving the display, you must write to the second window. As shown in the diagram below, the system has saved only the first two windows:

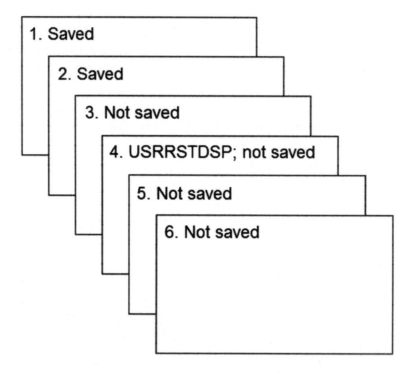

The USRRSTDSP keyword interacts with other keywords and window-related functions. Before using the keyword, you should understand the following points (assume that the USRRSTDSP keyword is in effect):

1. If a window record is written to a window that was saved (window 1 or 2 in the above example), the saved display is restored, the current record is written to the target window, and the target window becomes active. At this point, the USRRSTDSP keyword is no longer in effect.

2. If a window definition record is written to a window that was not saved (window 3, 4, or 5 in the above example), it becomes a new window. It's

merged with the previous display image and written to the display. No windows are removed.

3. If a window record is read from a window that was not saved (window 3, 4, or 5 in the above example), an error message is returned to the application.

4. If the initial display has been saved and the application writes to a window record specifying the RMVWDW keyword, any existing windows are removed. The new window is displayed on top of the initial display. The new window is active, and USRRSTDSP is no longer in effect.

5. If the initial display isn't saved and the application writes to a window record that specifies the RMVWDW keyword, all existing windows are removed. The new window is displayed on top of the initial display. The new window is active, and USRRSTDSP is still in effect.

6. If a non-window record is written to the display and USRRSTDSP is specified on the first window, then the window is not removed, and the non-window record may overlay all or part of the window.

Empowered with all this new knowledge, let's look at another example of a windowed subfile. In this example, I won't use USRRSTDSP, even though I'm coding under one of the conditions IBM recommends in the list above. I will allow IBM i to control the saving and restoring of the display for the purpose of this example—and because it does it so well. (If you're anxious to put USRRSTDSP to use, you'll see an example in Chapter 6, where I discuss side-by-side subfiles.) Also, while I'm telling you what I'm not going to do, I will mention that the following example does not use the RMVWDW keyword. I have nothing against this particular keyword, but I have no use for it in this example. Please feel free, though, to add a window to this display and check out the RMVWDW keyword on your own.

What Prompted You to Display?

In my experience, windowed subfiles are most widely used as prompting tools. If you need data that exists somewhere in a master file, why rekey it when you can look it up? Providing a user with a pop-up window to display and allow selection not only saves time but also helps avoid possible keying errors.

At *http://www.mc-store.com/5104.html*, I have provided the complete program (PNL001RG) and DDS (PNL001DF) that allows a user to key some data. In this program, the user can press the F4 key to get a pop-up window that lists names from a master file. By selecting a name, the user brings it back to the original display, to fill in the data entry screen.

Note that PNL001RG and PNL001DF are merely a simulated data entry program and an associated display file. I say "simulated" because they're really not doing anything. I coded only the beginnings to show you how the prompting and returning of data work. I didn't provide a full-fledged maintenance program—you already have that.

The window we'll be discussing isn't part of PNL001DF and PNL001RG. It's a separate program and display file. When you press F4, you're calling a new program to get your data. Many applications can benefit from this name-prompting tool, but if you make it a part of every program that needs it, you're setting yourself up for a nightmare of duplicate code. Instead, code the prompting program separately, to be used by other programs without duplication.

RTNCSRLOC and Prompting

Figure 4.8 shows the addition of the CF04 to the DDS, which makes F4 a valid function key. In this example, the user presses F4 to prompt for a name.

```
A                                      DSPSIZ(24 80 *DS3)

A                                      PRINT

A                                      ERRSFL

A                                      CA03

A                                      CA12

A                                      CF04
```

Figure 4.8: Adding the F4 key to allow prompting (PNL001DF).

Figure 4.9 introduces you to a new keyword, Return Cursor Location (RNTCSRLOC), which we added to the PANEL1 format. This keyword isn't subfile-specific, but it deserves mentioning. It's used to return the record format and field name that contain the cursor when control is returned to your program.

This keyword has several parameters and many uses, but mentioning them is outside our scope here. For this program, I'm really only interested in the field name. I want my RPG program to know which field the user was on when he or she pressed F4. The parameters &FLD and &RCD are defined in the record format as hidden, 10-byte, alpha fields. I'm not going to use this information in my example, but as we get into the RPG, this information will allow you to understand the flexibility afforded by this keyword.

```
A           R PANEL1

A                                         RTNCSRLOC(&RCD &FLD)

A                                       1  2'PNL001RG'

A           MODE         6A  O  2  2DSPATR(HI)

A                                       1 24'Subfile Program with Update      '

A                                         DSPATR(HI)

A                                       1 71DATE

A                                         EDTCDE(Y)

A                                       2 71TIME

A           RCD         10A  H

A           FLD         10A  H
```

Figure 4.9: An example of the RTNCSRLOC keyword, with hidden fields defined for the key and record (PNL001DF).

As I stated earlier, this isn't a full-fledged data entry program. I'm merely providing an example of how you might activate a window subfile in another program.

The code in Figure 4.10 shows a typical function-key interrogation routine. If F4 (represented by the prompt constant) is pressed, the Get_Data subroutine is executed.

```
Dou  *Inkc or *Inkl;  // Process until F3 or F12 is pressed.

  Exfmt Panel1;

  If  Cfkey = Prompt;

    Exsr Get_Data;

  Endif;

Enddo;
```

Figure 4.10: The code to prompt for a name when F4 is pressed (PNL001RG).

Figure 4.11 shows the Get_Data subroutine. When F4 is pressed, the program will call program SFL008RG (the windowed subfile) and pass one parameter. Nothing is sent to SFL008RG. The DBIDNM parameter is used only to hold the customer number of the name selected by the user. If there's something in DBIDNM upon returning from SFL008RG, it's used to chain to the data file and retrieve the appropriate information for the screen. Note that the CALL operation code is not supported in free-form RPG, so I was required to prototype the call to SFL008RG.

```
Begsr Get_Data;



CallP Get_The_Data (Dbidnm);      // Call the prompt program



If Dbidnm > 0;

  Chain Dbidnm Sfl001pf;

  If Not %found;

    Dblnam = error;

  Endif;

Endif;



Endsr;
```

Figure 4.11: The prompt window is actually a separate program, called from the Get_Data subroutine (PNL001RG).

In this example, there's only one prompting program to be called, SFL008RG. No matter which field your cursor is on, the name window will display when F4 is pressed. Suppose, however, that you have other data you wish to prompt for. How do you tell which prompting program to call? You could use the field name returned to the program by the RTNCSRLOC keyword. Depending on the field name returned, you could call a different prompting window.

Figure 4.12 shows how you could code the program if you wanted to call a different prompting program, depending on the field where the user placed the cursor before pressing F4. The first WHEN clause checks for the field DBFNAM, which is the first name field, and calls the original Get_Data subroutine. A second WHEN clause determines whether F4 was pressed on the first address field, DBADD1. If this clause is satisfied, another subroutine can be executed to call a different windowed subfile program. This type of structure can continue for as many fields as you want to prompt.

```
If  Cfkey = Prompt;

 Select;

   When Fld = 'DBFNAM';
     Exsr Get_Data;

   When Fld = 'DBADD1';
     Exsr Some_Other_Routine;
```

Figure 4.12: A method to tell your program which prompting program to call based on where the cursor resides (PNL001RG).

Selection Lists—A Cool Way to Return Data

Now let's take a look at the actual windowed subfile for this example. After all, that's why you're reading this chapter, isn't it? SFL008DF is the DDS for the windowed subfile that will be called from PNL001RG. This DDS uses some additional window keywords mentioned earlier in this chapter, as well as a few of the subfile keywords introduced in Chapter 1.

In this example, instead of providing the user with a simple load-all subfile from which to choose data, I add a twist. That twist is in the form of a selection list. A selection-list subfile is perfect for prompting and returning data. What differentiates a selection-list subfile from a regular subfile is its ability to restrict the user to one choice, or allow many choices. With a selection list, you can also allow simple cursor maneuvering and data selection without adding an input field. (You'll understand more on this point as you continue.) To make this subfile a selection list, I employ two of the subfile selection list keywords introduced in Chapter 1.

Designing the Selection List

You've seen most of the DDS for this example before. It's a load-all subfile, since SFLSIZ and SFLPAG are not equal. You'll also notice that there is no ROLLUP or ROLLDOWN keyword—another indication that this is a load-all subfile. Once again, take data file size into consideration before employing this type of subfile. (See Chapter 2 for more information.)

Figure 4.13 shows the subfile window record format in which I define a one-byte hidden field, CTLFLD, and assign it as the selection-list choice-control field, with the SFLCHCCTL keyword. Coding it this way enables the OS to ensure that the selection list rules, which are determined later in my control record format, are enforced. I also define another hidden field, DBIDNM, which is my customer number. It won't be displayed, but I'll pass it back to the calling program when the user makes a selection.

```
A           R WINDOW1                    SFL
A*
A           CTLFLD          1Y 0H        SFLCHCCTL
A           DBIDNM      R       H        REFFLD(PFR/DBIDNM *LIB/SFL001PF)
A           FULLNM         40   0  6  2
```

Figure 4.13: A windowed subfile in which IBM i enforces the logic rules for the user (SFL008DF).

The last field is a 40-byte alpha field called FULLNM. This field will house the first and last name from the data file. I decided to concatenate the two fields because of a restriction with selection lists, which dictates that you can have only one output field when a selection list is used. Because I want both names to be displayed in the window, I concatenate them into one field. Clever, huh?

Take a look at my window keywords in the code in Figure 4.14. This code is in the definition of the subfile control record format, WINDOW1. You've already seen the WINDOW keyword, but it's a little different here.

```
A                                  WINDOW(*DFT 14 44 *NOMSGLIN)

A                                  WDWBORDER((*COLOR PNK))

A                                  WDWTITLE((*TEXT 'Name Selection') (-

A                                  *COLOR WHT))

A                                  WDWTITLE((*TEXT 'F12=Cancel') (*COL-

A                                  OR BLU) *BOTTOM)
```

Figure 4.14: The keywords that define where the window will appear and how it will look (SFL008DF).

Instead of hard-coded coordinates for starting positions, I use the parameter *DFT. This will allow my window to display in relation to where the cursor is located. If the cursor is at the top of the screen when F4 is pressed, the window will display underneath the cursor. If the cursor is at the bottom, the window will display above it. I define the window as 14 lines long and 44 characters wide and tell it that I don't need a message line.

The next window keyword is WDWBORDER, which defines the borders of the window. I used the default borders in my last example, so I didn't have to explicitly define it. You can define the characters, color, and attributes of your window. This example uses the default characters and attributes, but changes the color to pink. (It's my wife's favorite color, okay?) Because it's so simple, this is one keyword I like to define in SDA.

The next keyword can't be defined using SDA, so don't waste your time. The WDWTITLE keyword allows you to insert text into your border. The text can be placed on the top or bottom and can be aligned on the left, center, or right. However, note that some workstation controllers don't support bottom border titles or non-centered top border titles. You can code for them, and if your controller doesn't support them, they'll be ignored. My first border title is type *TEXT, centered on the top and colored white. Because centered and *TOP are the defaults for this keyword, I didn't explicitly define them.

The second WDWBORDER keyword allows me to add text to the bottom of my border. Because I can't add a separate record format to display the valid function keys, as I can with a regular subfile, I need another way to accomplish this. A bottom window border is that way. I add the *TEXT data "F12=Cancel," color it blue, and place it in the bottom border of the window. Because left-justified placement is the default for bottom window borders, I don't have to explicitly define it.

Let's pause for a moment to look at a fact I quickly brushed over: I can't have a function-key record format. Each record format in which I add the WINDOW keyword becomes a window. If I create a record format to display function keys without the WINDOW keyword, it will be written to the original display. If I add the WINDOW keyword or reference a format with the WINDOW keyword, it becomes its own window. Therefore, the only way to show the user the function keys at the bottom of the window is to do so in the border.

Figure 4.15 illustrates the two keywords that are important to this selection list. These are also part of the definition of the subfile control record format, WINDOW1.

A	SFLSNGCHC(*RSTCSR)
A	SFLCSRRRN(&RRN1)

Figure 4.15: These keywords provide a single choice list for the user (SFL008DF).

The first important keyword is the Subfile Single Choice (SFLSNGCHC) keyword, which tells the OS that only one choice can be selected and returned from the list. The user can scroll through and try to select many entries, but only the last entry selected is returned when Enter is pressed. The Restrict Cursor (*RSTCSR) parameter restricts the cursor to the list, so the user can use the arrow keys to scroll down the current page without leaving the list. When the cursor reaches the bottom of the list, it automatically goes back to the top.

The Subfile Cursor Relative Record Number (SFLCSRRRN) keyword and its parameter return the subfile relative record number the cursor is on when control is returned back to the RPG program. The &RRN1 parameter is defined as a hidden field of five, zoned decimal. Your program will use the relative record number to send the correct information back to the calling program.

Earlier in this chapter, you saw how to display a window over a record format in the same display file by using the OVERLAY keyword. In this example, we want to display a window over a record format in a different display file. OVERLAY will not work in this case.

To display a new window without erasing the current display, use the ASSUME keyword. The ASSUME keyword tells IBM i to assume that the record is already written when the display file is open. As a result, IBM i won't attempt to erase the current display before displaying the window. Ironically, you can't use the ASSUME and WINDOW keywords in the same record format.

Because of this, I create the record shown in Figure 4.16, called ASSUME, with the ASSUME keyword and one non-display field. I never have to reference this record in my RPG, but I can write the window without erasing the current display by placing it in my DDS. (It's now our little secret how to fool IBM i.)

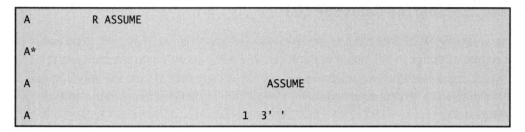

```
A               R ASSUME

A*

A                                       ASSUME

A                                 1  3'  '
```

Figure 4.16: The ASSUME keyword allows the user to display one program's window over another without erasing the current display (SFL008DF).

Figure 4.17 shows what the window looks like when the user presses F4 from PNL001RG.

```
PNL001RG             Subfile Program with Update          2/07/11
                                                          06:58:14


   Customer Number . : 0000000

   First Name. . . . . _____
                        ┌─────────── Name Selection ────────────┐
   Last Name . . . . . │                                        │
                        │ Position to desired record, press Enter.│
   Middle Initial. . . │ Press F12 to return without a selection.│
                        │                                        │
   Nick Name . . . . . │ Last Name          First Name          │
                        │ ▌Anthony           Tony              ▐ │
   Address Line 1. . . │ Baker              Ana                 │
                        │ Bilog              Frances             │
   Address Line 2. . . │ Blade              Billy               │
                        │ Capacino           Tony                │
   Address Line 3. . . │ Fleischer          Jim                 │
                        │ Gandalf            Norm                │
                        │                              More...   │
                        │                                        │
                        └ F12=Cancel ════════════════════════════┘
   F3=Exit   F4=Prompt    F12=Cancel
```

Figure 4.17: An example of a selection-list subfile.

Programming the Selection List

As usual, the DDS does most of the work for the selection list. However, there are a couple of things to talk about in the RPG. The RPG doesn't care whether you're using a regular subfile or a selection-list subfile. As a matter of fact, the only hint you get that this is a selection list—and it's a slight hint at that—is found in the code in Figure 4.18.

```
// Load data to subfile


Setll (*Loval) Sfl0011f;

Dou %eof;           // Read while there are records in the file.

  Read Sfl0011f;

  If Not %eof;

    Rrn1 = Rrn1 + 1;  // Increment subfile record number.

    Fullnm = Dblnam + Dbfnam;

    Write Window1;    // Write the record to the window.

  Endif;

Enddo;
```

Figure 4.18: Because selection-list subfiles can only contain one field, I concatenate first and last names into the FULLNM field (SFL008RG).

The fact that I concatenate the first and last names into FULLNM doesn't guarantee that this is a selection list, but it's the closest thing to a clue. Other than that, the load-all routine works like the others you've seen so far in this book. The main routine clears the subfile, loads it, and then displays it. I don't even bother with a **DOW** or **DOU** loop because control only needs to be passed back to the program once before returning to the calling program. The user will either select a record and press Enter, or press F12 to cancel. In either case, the program only needs one pass through it. If the user scrolls through the subfile, that scrolling will be handled by IBM i—but you already knew that, didn't you?

Figure 4.19 shows what happens when control is passed back to the program. If F3 and F12 are not pressed, the program CHAINs to the WINDOW1 subfile record format with the relative record number returned by the RTNCSRLOC keyword. By chaining to the subfile, I can get the customer number (DBIDNM) of the selected record and pass it back to the calling program. If F3 or F12 is pressed, the ELSE clause is executed, which zeros out the customer number before returning to the calling program. Looking back at PNL001RG, you'll see that it checks whether DBIDNM is greater than zero before it does anything else.

```
If (Not *Inkc) And (Not *Inkl);

  Chain Rrn1 Window1;

  Id_Num = Dbidnm;

Else;

  Id_Num = 0;

Endif;
```

Figure 4.19: This logic gets the information from the subfile record selected by the user, to pass back to the calling program (SFL008RG).

There you have it. There's not much to the RPG in this example. All the new stuff was in the DDS. However, you have learned that, with very little code, you can provide your users with a very effective way to display and return data from a pop-up window.

Summary

The following are the high-level concepts and new keywords you should take from this chapter:

- Windowed subfiles are relatively easy to create because all the work is done in the DDS.
- Without changing the RPG, you can make it control a windowed subfile that was converted from a regular subfile.
- Selection-list subfiles offer additional selection-control criteria and cursor movement within the subfile.
- IBM i handles all the save and restore processing when windows are written to the display.
- You can disable the save and restore processing by using the USRRSTDSP keyword.
- The ASSUME keyword cannot be used in the same format as the WINDOW keyword, but it's paramount if you want to display a window from a called program over a display, without first erasing that display.

CHAPTER 5

MESSAGE SUBFILES:
WHAT'S THAT PLUS SIGN NEXT TO MY
MESSAGE?

Message subfiles are special subfiles designed to hold—you guessed it—messages. Message subfiles have some unique properties that make them very useful, loading themselves automatically from messages on a given program message queue. (We'll talk more about program message queues in a bit.)

Message subfiles also allow users to view the second-level help text associated with a message—without any additional programming effort. Message subfiles make it possible to set up a consistent group of information, warning, or error messages in a message file for a given program or application and display those messages to the user with the greatest of ease. Well, at least with some ease. With just a little direction from your RPG and DDS, message subfiles pretty much take care of themselves.

Message Subfile Ground Rules

In general, here's how you use a message subfile:

1. Set up a message file (*MSGF) containing the messages you want to use in your application. You can use an existing message file, or create your own. You shouldn't usually modify system-supplied message files, such as QCPFMSG.

Message files are created with the CRTMSGF command. New messages can be added via the ADDMSGD command or the WRKMSGF command.

2. Define a message subfile in your display file.

3. Code your application program to send program messages to the program message queue. The best way to accomplish this in RPG is to use the Send Program Message (QMHSNDPM) application programming interface (API). You can also use the SNDPGMMSG command, although the best place to use that command is in a CL program.

4. After displaying the message subfile, clear the messages from the program message queue using the Remove Program Message (QMHRMVPM) API. You can also use the RMVMSG command from a CL program. Never fear—I'll show you how to display message subfiles using CL.

There are a couple of things you should know before we move on. First, every call stack entry—which can be an OPM program or an ILE procedure—has a corresponding program message queue with the same name, as shown in Table 5.1. This is important to know, especially when you start dealing with ILE and multiple call stack entries. Second, the program status data structure in RPG has fields that contain the program name and the procedure name. Third, don't worry if you're not familiar with APIs. I'll go through all you need to know to use the two message-handling APIs mentioned earlier.

Table 5.1: Call Stack Entries and Associated Program Message Queues	
Call Stack Entry	**Program Message Queue**
QCMD	QCMD
OPMPGM1	OPMPGM1
ILEPROC1	ILEPROC1
ILEPROC2	ILEPROC2

Program Status Data Structure—Procedure Name

The source code in Figure 5.1 shows that the program status data structure in RPG has fields that contain the program name and the procedure name. This saves you from having to hard-code the program name in your Send and Remove APIs. It also frees you from some extra coding in your program (as if message subfiles aren't doing enough for you already). You'll see more about this as we get into the code. As usual, the complete code listings are included at *http://www.mc-store.com/5104.html*.

Figure 5.1: The program status data structure is useful for retrieving a program message queue name.

Message-Handling APIs

APIs are simply callable programs (or, in some cases, procedures) supplied to you by a software vendor (IBM, in this case) that allow you to perform low-level or complex functions. Programmers often shy away from APIs because of their sometimes-complicated interfaces, but if you're willing to brave new worlds and give them a try, you'll find a wealth of programming power just waiting to be tapped.

More on Program Message Queues

I created my own message file for this chapter, but you can certainly use the system-supplied messages and insert your own text. For instance, suppose users are accustomed to seeing message CPF9898 (from the system-supplied message file QCPFMSG) as something serious. You could still use that message ID and substitute it with your own message. This doesn't mean you change the CPF9898 message in the actual message file. Rather, you override the message text in your program. If there are substitution parameters associated with a specific message, you can also fill in those parameters using the program message APIs. If message files aren't your thing, you can also send text messages to the program message queue and use no message file at all.

That about covers it. Now, let's look at some code!

The Same, But Different

In my example, I've set up two messages, SFL0001 and SFL0002, in a message file called SFLMSGQ. SFL009DF is a display file that demonstrates the use of message subfiles. It consists of three record formats: SCREEN1, MSGSFL, and MSGCTL. SCREEN1, the primary screen, allows the user to enter data. As you'll see in the RPG program (SFL009RG), this data isn't going anywhere; its purpose is purely to demonstrate how to use a message subfile.

MSGSFL is the message subfile record format, and MSGCTL is the control format for MSGSFL. Because they work together to control the workings of the subfile, these formats act much like the SF1CTL and SFL1 formats you've seen throughout this book. There are, however, some differences between regular subfiles and message subfiles.

With regular subfiles, you have to handle the loading and clearing in your program. In your RPG program, you'll typically set on the indicator used to condition the SFLCLR keyword in your DDS, write to the subfile control format (SF1CTL, in most examples in this book), and set off the indicator to get ready to load and display. With message subfiles, you don't explicitly clear the subfile in your program. Instead, you link the subfile to a program message queue and remove messages from that message queue. This, in essence, clears the subfile.

This same theory holds true for loading the subfile. When displaying subfile records in a regular subfile, you must first execute some sort of load routine. This usually consists of a DO loop that reads records from a database file and writes them to the subfile record format. Message subfiles will have none of that. By linking the message subfile to a specific program message queue and sending messages to that queue, the message subfile will automatically load itself with records from the program message queue.

Message subfiles require the use of several special DDS keywords. Let's look at the message subfile record in SFL009DF, shown in Figure 5.2, to see how they're arranged.

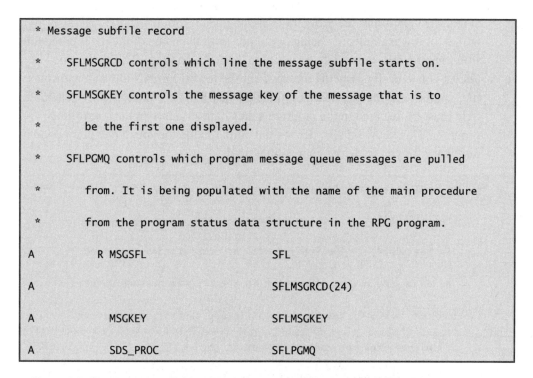

```
* Message subfile record

*     SFLMSGRCD controls which line the message subfile starts on.

*     SFLMSGKEY controls the message key of the message that is to

*        be the first one displayed.

*     SFLPGMQ controls which program message queue messages are pulled

*        from. It is being populated with the name of the main procedure

*        from the program status data structure in the RPG program.
A              R MSGSFL                    SFL
A                                          SFLMSGRCD(24)
A              MSGKEY                       SFLMSGKEY
A              SDS_PROC                     SFLPGMQ
```

Figure 5.2: The format keywords for the message subfile record in SFL009DF.

In the message subfile record format (MSGSFL), shown in Figure 5.3, the following keywords are required:

- **SFLMSGRCD** sets the starting line on the display for the message subfile. In most cases, it's set to 24 (the bottom line of the display), although you could display more than one message at a time. In that case, you would set this parameter accordingly.

- **SFLMSGKEY** controls the message key of the first message to be displayed in the message subfile. Every message on a message queue has a unique key assigned to it as it arrives on the queue. In certain cases, you might wish to maintain old messages on the queue and only display messages from a certain point forward in the message subfile. Setting the message key allows you to control which messages are displayed.

- **SFLPGMQ** determines the program message queue from which the messages are pulled. In my example, it's being populated with the name of the main procedure from the program status data structure in the RPG program. This technique allows you to easily copy the message subfile record formats into a new display file, without making any changes to the display file. Of course, the SDS_PROC field must be declared in the program status data structure in the controlling program. This keyword also defines the output fields for you. No explicit code is necessary for you to define your subfile fields.

```
* Message subfile control record

*     SFLPAG > SFLSIZ to allow the system to control page up and down

*         in the subfile.  The subfile will be automatically extended

*         based on the number of entries in the program message queue.

*     SFLDSP and SFLDSPCTL cause the subfile and control record to be

*         displayed when the control format is thrown

*     SFLINZ, in this case, causes the system to automatically load

*         the subfile with messages from the message queue specified

*     SFLPGMQ controls which program message queue messages are pulled

*         from. It is being populated with the name of the main procedure

*         from the program status data structure in the RPG program.

*     SFLEND with indicators that always evaluate to TRUE, allows the

*         system to automatically toggle the "+" sign that indicates if

*         there are more records to display in the subfile.

A          R MSGCTL                       SFLCTL(MSGSFL)
```

Continued

A		SFLSIZ(2)
A		SFLPAG(1)
A		SFLDSP
A		SFLDSPCTL
A		SFLINZ
A N99		SFLEND
A	SDS_PROC	SFLPGMQ

Figure 5.3: The format keywords in the message subfile control record (SFL009DF).

The SFLCTL, SFLSIZ, SFLPAG, SFLDSP, SFLDSPCTL, and SFLEND keywords behave normally in a message subfile, except that SFLDSP and SFLDSPCTL must be used without conditioning indicators. Also, SFLPAG must be at least one less than SFLSIZ in a message subfile; the two keywords cannot be equal.

Message subfiles are considered load-all subfiles. Notice that I don't use the *MORE parameter on my message subfile. Using this parameter causes "More . . ." and "Bottom" to display one line under the last line on the display. Because I'm using line 24, which is the last possible line on the display, I would get an error if I tried to use the *MORE parameter. The plus sign works for me, but if you're dying to use *MORE with your message subfiles, try starting on line 23 with SFLMSGRCD(23) and keeping SFLPAG as one, so you won't get an error.

Let's look at the differences in how two of the keywords behave when they're in a message subfile:

- **SFLINZ**, in the case of a message subfile, causes the system to automatically load the subfile with messages from the specified message queue. This is different from its use in regular subfiles. Remember, in regular subfiles, SFLINZ loads the subfile with the number of records indicated by SFLSIZ and sets the fields to their default values.

- **SFLPGMQ** is used to control the program from which message-queue messages are pulled. It's populated with the name of the main procedure from the program status data structure in the RPG program. It might seem redundant to use this keyword in both formats, but it really, really isn't. Specifying this keyword in the subfile record format allows you to link the subfile to a specific program message queue, which allows you to clear and possibly load the subfile by controlling the program message queue. However, it's the SFLPGMQ keyword entry in the subfile control format that allows you to automatically load the subfile. If you don't specify it in the subfile control format, you'll need to code the load routine in your program. Always use this keyword in the subfile control format. This is one case where redundancy causes efficiency.

The RPG

The RPG is basically used to control SCREEN1. It doesn't have any direct contact with the message subfile. The RPG program sends messages to, and removes messages from, the program message queue. It also helps the message subfile link to the program message queue by retrieving the message queue name from the program data structure and sharing it with the display file. As you will soon see, however, it doesn't directly load, clear, or display the subfile.

Take a look at Figure 5.1 again. The program status data structure provides information about the program, just as a file information data structure provides information about a specific file. In my example, I want to retrieve the procedure name associated with this program. I can get this by specifying the keyword *PROC. I'll the define SDS_PROC to associate with the *PROC keyword. Notice that this is the same name I used in my DDS. By doing this, I can pass the name of the procedure, and subsequently the program message queue name, to the display file, and allow it to link the program message queue to the message subfile. I also specified the program name, which can be retrieved from positions 334 through 343. I'm not going to use that field in my example, but I'm showing you that it's there in case you choose to use it.

Figure 5.4 shows the fields I'll use as parameters to call the message-handling APIs. You'll see more about these fields when I get to the API call statements. They are the D specs from RPG program SFL009RG.

```
*** Procedure prototype declaration

*       Think of this as the PLIST in the CALLING procedure

D  MsgId          s            7A

D  MsgLoc         s           20A   Inz('SFLMSGF    *LIBL    ')

D  MsgRplDta      s            1A   Inz(' ')

D  MsgRplDtaLen   s           4B 0  Inz(0)

D  MsgType        s           10A   Inz('*DIAG')

D  MsgQueue       s          276A   Inz('*')

D  MsgCallStack   s           4B 0  Inz(0)

D  MsgKey         s            4A   Inz(' ')

D  MsgErr         s           4B 0  Inz(0)

D  Msgrmv         s           10A   Inz('*ALL')
```

Figure 5.4: The D specs used to call the message APIs in SFL009RG.

The mainline of the RPG, shown in Figure 5.5, is simply a DOU loop that processes SCREEN1. It performs a WRITE to the message subfile control format, MSGCTL, before SCREEN1 is written to allow the user to enter some data. This WRITE causes the message subfile to be loaded with any messages that exist in the program message queue and then be written to the screen. The first time through, I haven't sent any messages to the program message queue. As a result, the message subfile is empty.

```
/Free


  Dou (Cfkey = Exit) Or (Cfkey = Cancel);

    Write Msgctl;

    Exfmt Screen1;

    MsgKey = *Blanks;

    Exsr Rcvmsg;



    Select;


    When Cfkey = Enter;

      If First_Name <> 'Kevin';

        Msgid = 'SFL0001';

        Exsr Sndmsg;

      Endif;
```

Continued

```
      If Last_Name <> 'Vandever';

        Msgid = 'SFL0002';

        Exsr Sndmsg;

      Endif;



    Endsl;



  Enddo;



  *Inlr = *on;



/End-Free
```

Figure 5.5: The mainline of program SFL009RG.

The initial screen lets the user enter a first and last name. When the Enter key is pressed, the RPG program interrogates the names and determines whether a message should be sent. In my example, if the user doesn't enter "Kevin" as the first name, message ID "SFL0001" is moved to the MSGID field, and the SNDMSG subroutine is executed. If "Vandever" isn't entered as the last name, MSGID is evaluated to "SFL0002," and SNDMSG is executed again. (We'll cover this subroutine in more detail later in this chapter.)

Each time the SNDMSG subroutine is executed, a message is written to the program message queue and displayed to the screen when the WRITE operation is performed. Because I want the messages removed after they've been displayed, the first thing the code does upon returning from SCREEN1 is execute the RMVMSG subroutine. This clears the program message queue, and subsequently the message subfile, for the next interrogation of data.

Figure 5.6 shows what happens when the user enters the first name correctly, but misspells the last name. Once the user corrects the last name and presses Enter, the message disappears.

```
                        Message Subfile Example


     Type a First and Last Name and Press Enter to test the Message Subfile.


          Enter First Name . . Kevin

          Enter Last Name. . . Vandeverhoof









     F3=Exit   F12=Cancel

 Last name should be Vandever
```

Figure 5.6: The single error message for a misspelled last name.

Figure 5.7 shows the reward for spelling the name correctly: no error messages.

```
                         Message Subfile Example


      Type a First and Last Name and Press Enter to test the Message Subfile.


          Enter First Name . . Kevin_____

          Enter Last Name. . . Vandever_____







   F3=Exit    F12=Cancel
```

Figure 5.7: No error messages.

If the user spells both names incorrectly, two messages are written to the program message queue. Now, when the message subfile is displayed on the screen, you'll see the first message with a plus sign at the far right side, signifying more records, as shown in Figure 5.8. If you place your cursor on the subfile record and press Page Down to get the next record, you'll see the second error message, shown in Figure 5.9.

```
                         Message Subfile Example


      Type a First and Last Name and Press Enter to test the Message Subfile.


          Enter First Name . . Kevinnnn_____

          Enter Last Name. . . Vandeverrrr_____









    F3=Exit    F12=Cancel

  First Name should be kevin                                          +
```

Figure 5.8: The first of two error messages.

If you're using a message file and have added second-level help for your messages, you can see those second-level messages by placing the cursor on the message subfile record and pressing the Help key. Figure 5.10 shows the results of pressing Help on the second message in the subfile.

```
                          Message Subfile Example


      Type a First and Last Name and Press Enter to test the Message Subfile.


          Enter First Name . . Kevinnnn_____

          Enter Last Name. . . Vandeverrrr_____










     F3=Exit   F12=Cancel

Last name should be Vandever
```

Figure 5.9: The second of two error messages.

```
  _               Additional Message Information

  Message ID . . . . . . :   SFL0001     Severity . . . . . . . . :   00
  Message type . . . . . :   Diagnostic
  Date sent  . . . . . . :   02/16/11    Time sent  . . . . . . :   05:05:04

  Message . . . . :   First Name should be kevin
  Kevin is a very nice guy but really likes it when people spell his first name
    correctly







                                                                       Bottom
  Press Enter to continue.

  F3=Exit   F6=Print   F9=Display message details
  F10=Display messages in job log   F12=Cancel   F21=Select assistance level
```

Figure 5.10: A display of second-level help for an error message.

You can search all day for the extra code that allows this feature, but you won't find it. That's because it's taken care of by the operating system. I think you should take a moment now to thank IBM i and message subfiles for making your life so much easier.

QMHSNDPM

Let's take a look at what is essentially my subfile load routine. The SNDMSG subroutine is executed whenever I need to send a message to the program message queue. To accomplish this task, I use the QMHSNDPM message-handling API, as shown in Figure 5.11.

```
C     sndmsg        begsr


C                   call      'QMHSNDPM'

C                   parm                    msgId

C                   parm                    msgLoc

C                   parm                    msgRplDta

C                   parm                    msgRplDtaLen

C                   parm                    msgType

C                   parm                    msgQueue

C                   parm                    msgCallStack

C                   parm                    msgKey

C                   parm                    msgErr


C                   endsr
```

Figure 5.11: The API to send a message to the program's message queue in SFL009RG.

You don't have to use this API to send program messages. Instead, you could write a CL program that uses the SNDPGMMSG command, and call that program. Alternatively, you could use the QCMDEXC API to run the Send Program Message (SNDPGMMSG) command from your RPG. To me, when working with RPG, the cleanest and most efficient method is to use the message APIs directly, instead of using QCMDEXC to run the SNDPGMMSG command. However, when coding in CL, it's much easier to work directly with the SNDPGMMSG command and skip the use of APIs.

Now let's talk about the parameters. There are nine required parameters associated with the QMHSNDPM API. There are also four optional parameters, but that's all I am going to say about them. The following is a list of the parameters I use in my program, with a brief explanation of each one:

- **MSGID** contains the seven-byte message identification. This field is associated with the message identifier in the message file. If you are not using a message file, this field will be blank.
- **MSGLOC** qualifies the message file associated with the message ID in the first parameter. The first 10 positions of this field will contain the name of the message file, and the last 10 will contain the library. The keywords *LIBL and *CURLIB may be used instead of a library. If the MSGID parameter is blank, this parameter should also be blank.
- **MSGRPLDTA** is a variable-length character field or pointer used in a few different ways. If a message identifier is specified, this parameter specifies the data that's inserted in the predefined message's substitution variables.

    You've seen that before. It's when a message and a program name or statement number appears embedded in the message. If your messages contain substitution variables, you'll use this to fill those parameters with helpful information. If blanks are used for the message identifier, this parameter specifies the complete text of an immediate message. In my example, I want to use the message text exactly as it reads in the message file. To do this, I define this parameter as a one-byte character field and initialize it to blank—more specifically, I don't use it.
- **MSGRPLDTALEN** tells the API the length of the previous parameter. For example, if you were sending 70-byte messages using the MSGRPLDTA parameter, the parameter would be set to 70. In my example, I'm not using it, so I set it to zero.

- **MSGTYPE** defines the type of message to send. In my example, I'm sending diagnostic messages (*DIAG), but you could also send informational, completion, escape, notify, inquiry, request, and status messages.
- **MSGQUEUE** is the program message queue call stack to which I send the messages. I used the reserved value of an asterisk (*) because I'm sending to the current call stack entry—the one in which this procedure is running.

  This parameter is 276 bytes long because of ILE. You could have many nested procedures in your application, and this parameter allows you to explicitly qualify them by name, separated by colons. The last 20 bytes are reserved for the module and program name of the nested procedures. My program, procedure, and module are known by the same name, and because I'm sending to the current call stack, I only need the asterisk.
- **MSGCALLSTACK** tells the API on what level in the call stack to look for the entry named in the previous parameter. In my case, because I'm using the current call stack, I set this parameter to zero. If you wanted to send a message to an entry in the previous call stack, you would set this parameter to one.
- **MSGKEY** is the key to messages being sent. Because I want all messages to be sent, displayed, and removed, I set this to blanks.
- **MSGERR** is the name of the data structure that returns error information. I don't remember ever getting any errors in my life, so I set this to blanks and don't use it.

That's how I use the parameters in the QHMSNDPM API in my example. If you're planning to implement a true RPG IV/ILE application, I suggest you check out IBM's message-handling API documentation. It will give you a more complete understanding of this API and how it's used in the ILE. (You can perform an internet search on "IBM message-handling API documentation" for additional information.)

QMHRMVPM

You've seen how to send messages, which also builds the subfile. Now let's take a look at how to remove messages, which also clears the subfile. I use the QMHRMVPM API for this task, as shown in Figure 5.12.

```
C       rcvmsg      begsr


C                   call      'QMHRMVPM'

C                   parm                    msgQueue

C                   parm                    msgCallStack

C                   parm                    msgKey

C                   parm                    msgRmv

C                   parm                    msgErr



C                   endsr
```

Figure 5.12: The API to receive a message from the program's message queue (SFL009RG).

This API contains five required and four optional parameters. I'm not going to touch on the optional parameters in my example. Again, if you plan to implement a true RPG IV/ILE application, complete with subprocedures, service programs, and multiple activation groups, I suggest you read this API's documentation.

You've already seen four of the parameters because they're also used in the QMHSNDPM API, but they're worth mentioning again:

- The message queue, set to an asterisk to signify the current call stack
- The call stack level, set to zero again because I'm removing messages at the current call stack level
- The message key, set to blanks because I want to remove all message keys
- The name of the message error structure, which I don't use in this example

The only new parameter is MSGRMV. The MSGRMV parameter, which is actually the fourth parameter, tells which messages to remove. Because I want to remove all messages each time I call this API, I set this parameter to *ALL.

Still Not Sold?

What do you think of that? This simple RPG program contains no subfile code, but completely controls the contents of a subfile by sending and removing messages. I can understand that you might still be uncomfortable with the message-handling APIs. You like the simplicity of the SNDPGMMSG and RMVMSG commands. That's okay. You don't have to use them. As I said before, you can code a CL program that uses the commands to handle your program message queue and call that CL from your RPG program. You can also use the QCMDEXC API to run the commands from your RPG program. Another possible solution, depending on your application, is to control your screen and program message queue from a CL program.

CL to the Rescue

In case you're not aware of it, you can use a CL program to open a file. Note that I said *a* file, as in "one." If your application calls for you to open only one file, CL is a possible solution. There aren't many times when a display file is controlled in a CL program. Typically, a display file is used to display data from a database file.

With your newfound knowledge, you now understand that a CL program can't open both the display file and the database file. That disqualifies the CL program. However, there are times when you can use a CL program to control a display file. A good example is a menu. A menu doesn't usually use a database file, unless you store your menu option information in a database file—which is a great technique, by the way.

If you're displaying a menu or an entry screen, don't need a database or printer file to open, and want to use messages to communicate information to the user, employ a CL program. Coincidentally, I'm only opening one file in my example, the display file. So, let's convert it to the CL program SFL009CL, as shown in Figure 5.13.

```
            PGM


            DCLF       FILE(SFL009DF) RCDFMT(*ALL)

            CHGVAR     VAR(&SDS_PROC) VALUE('SFL009CL')

START:      SNDF       DEV(*FILE) RCDFMT(MSGCTL)

            SNDRCVF    DEV(*FILE) RCDFMT(SCREEN1)

            RMVMSG     MSGQ(*PGMQ) CLEAR(*ALL)


            IF         COND(&IN03 = '1' *OR &IN12 = '1') THEN(GOTO +

                         CMDLBL(END))


            IF         COND(&FIRST_NAME *NE 'Kevin') THEN(DO)

            SNDPGMMSG  MSGID(SFL0001) MSGF(SFLMSGF) TOPGMQ(*SAME)

            ENDDO
```

Continued

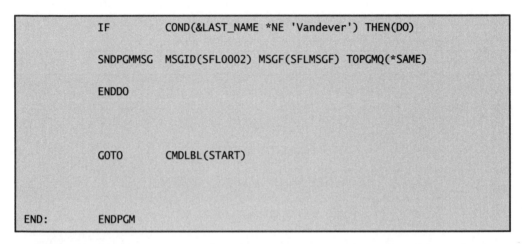

```
         IF          COND(&LAST_NAME *NE 'Vandever') THEN(DO)

         SNDPGMMSG   MSGID(SFL0002) MSGF(SFLMSGF) TOPGMQ(*SAME)

         ENDDO



         GOTO        CMDLBL(START)


END:     ENDPGM
```

Figure 5.13: Controlling the display file and the program message file from a CL program (SFL009CL).

How simple is that? It only takes about 16 lines of executable code. The first thing I do is declare the file and all its formats using the DCLF command. Notice that I use the same display file as before. Next comes the only real trick to this technique. In the RPG program, I used the program data structure to provide the program message queue name, but I don't have that luxury in CL. Instead, I'll have to physically move the appropriate procedure name (which has the same name as the program message queue) to the SDS_PROC field defined in my DDS. Then, I use the SNDF command to load the message subfile and display it. The SNDF command is equivalent to the RPG WRITE operation code.

Once I write the message subfile, I write the SCREEN1 format and read from it using the SNDRCVF command. This command is comparable to the RPG EXFMT command. I perform the same data interrogation I did in my RPG program, but instead of using the APIs to remove and send messages, I use the CL commands.

I admit that the commands are much easier to use. Give this technique a whirl, and prompt (F4) on the RMVMSG and SNDPGMMSG commands. You'll notice parameters that coincide with the API parameters. If nothing else, learning the APIs will help you better understand the CL commands.

Summary

Using the program message queue to communicate with the user provides a lot of flexibility. Add the wizardry of message subfiles, and you're on your way toward creating a killer application—and you haven't even started coding the business logic yet!

6

DISPLAYING MULTIPLE SUBFILES ON A SCREEN

In Chapter 1, I explained that a maximum of 24 subfiles can be active at one time and that a maximum of 12 can be displayed on a base screen or a window at one time. Don't remember? Go ahead and take another look. I'll wait. . . . See, I told you. Would I lie to you?

Anyway, in this chapter, you'll learn how to display more than one subfile on a screen. The example in this chapter involves displaying just two subfiles at once. However, you can use the provided explanation to help you display up to 12. Once you understand the basic concepts, your only challenge with adding more subfiles is figuring out where to put them.

Multiple Lists of Data

There are many situations where you might want to display more than one subfile on a screen. For instance, suppose you want to present information about an item. You might display one subfile showing the open orders for a given item, and another subfile on the same screen showing the open purchase orders for that item. A third subfile on the same screen might display the inventory status of that item from each warehouse.

You can see that this one screen would pack plenty of data for the user to digest. Add the ability to drill down and view the details of the subfile records (a skill you've acquired from reading previous chapters), and you've created a very powerful and useful inquiry application.

Horizontal or Vertical?

There are two ways to display multiple subfiles on a screen. One is the over/under method, where one subfile is on top of the other. Figure 6.1 shows a screen with two active subfiles, one on top of the other.

```
 SFL014RG              Multiple Subfiles - Over/Under          2/18/11
                                                              06:20:39
 _   First Name         MI        Last Name
     Tony               A         Anthony
     Ana                C         Baker
     Frances            X         Bilog
     Billy              B         Blade
     Tony               K         Capacino
     Jim                R         Fleischer
     Norm               A         Gandalf
                                                         More...

     First Name         MI        Last Name
     Tony               A         Anthony
     Ana                C         Baker
     Frances            X         Bilog
     Billy              B         Blade
     Tony               K         Capacino
     Jim                R         Fleischer
     Norm               A         Gandalf
                                                         More...
  F3=Exit    F12=Cancel
```

Figure 6.1: An example of the over/under subfile method.

Notice the two "More . . ." constants, indicating that each subfile has more records to display. That's the first clue that there's more than one subfile on the screen. The other clues are the space between the lists and the change in column headings.

The second method of presenting multiple subfiles is to display them side by side. This method is a little trickier because of the way in which subfiles occupy space on a screen. The basic technique is to use windows. Figure 6.2 shows an example of side-by-side subfiles using windows without borders.

```
 SFL014RG              Multiple Subfiles - Side by Side          2/18/11
                                                                06:23:00


   -

        First Name           MI              Last Name
        Tony                 A               Anthony
        Ana                  C               Baker
        Frances              X               Bilog
        Billy                B               Blade
        Tony                 K               Capacino
        Jim                  R               Fleischer
        Norm                 A               Gandalf
        Ezikiel              U               Hezikia
        Antwain              F               Jamison
        Coker                W               Jim
                          More...                         More...




   F3=Exit    F9=Toggle    F12=Cancel
```

Figure 6.2: An example of side-by-side subfiles using the windows method.

We're going to look at both methods. Let's start with the easier, or at least more intuitive, first: the over/under method.

Over/Under

Let's start with the DDS for this technique. (You can find the complete DDS, SFL015DF, at *http://www.mc-store.com/5104.html*.) As I mentioned earlier, this example involves displaying two subfiles on a screen.

My header simply displays a title line in row 1, the name of the program, and the date and time. My first subfile control record, shown in Figure 6.3, starts on line 3 and contains the column headings for the first, or top, subfile. Notice that this is a load-all subfile. In fact, I not only use the load-all technique in this example, but in all my multiple-subfile applications. I'll explain more about this later in this chapter.

My first subfile contains the first name, middle initial, and last name from an employee master file. It lists seven names per page. Nothing earth-shattering so far, right?

```
A           R SF1CTL                    SFLCTL(SFL1)

A                                       SFLSIZ(0050)

A                                       SFLPAG(0007)

A                                       OVERLAY

A   32                                  SFLDSP

A                                       SFLDSPCTL

A   31                                  SFLCLR

A   90                                  SFLEND(*MORE)

A             CURSOR        1  I  3  2DSPATR(ND)

A                              3  5'First Name'

A                                       DSPATR(HI)

A                              3 30'MI'

A                                       DSPATR(HI)

A                              3 37'Last Name'

A                                       DSPATR(HI)

A             RRN1         4S 0H        SFLRCDNBR
```

Figure 6.3: The subfile control record format for the top subfile in this over/under example.

The second subfile in the DDS is shown in Figure 6.4. It is identical to the first, except that the subfile control format starts on line 13, with the subfile record format directly under it at line 14, and the indicators are different. In my example, the subfiles are identical. This probably isn't what you would do in the real world, but for simplicity's sake, I'm displaying the same subfile two times, on the same screen.

```
A           R SF2CTL                    SFLCTL(SFL2)

A                                       SFLSIZ(0050)

A                                       SFLPAG(0007)

A                                       OVERLAY

A  42                                   SFLDSP

A                                       SFLDSPCTL

A  41                                   SFLCLR

A  90                                   SFLEND(*MORE)

A           CURSOR          1   I 13  2DSPATR(ND)

A                              13   5'First Name'

A                                       DSPATR(HI)

A                              13 30'MI'

A                                       DSPATR(HI)

A                              13 37'Last Name'

A                                       DSPATR(HI)

A           RRN2            4S 0H       SFLRCDNBR
```

Figure 6.4: The subfile control record format for the bottom subfile in this over/under example.

Finally, I define my function key format, FOOTER, to display the valid function keys available to the user. There you have the DDS for two subfiles defined on one screen, each containing seven records per page. Notice that I use two different sets of indicators for SFLCLR, SFLDSP, and SFLEND. This is simply so I can control the subfiles separately. Again, in the real world, you might have a case where one subfile has more records than the other. One or both might even be empty. In my example, however, they'll always be equal.

The (Tab) Key to Success

Before moving on to the RPG, I would like to explain another technique I use with over/under subfiles. Notice that each of the subfile control formats contains an input only (I) field, CURSOR, placed before the first column heading. This field has been defined as non-display (DSPATR(ND)) because I don't want to have it displayed on the screen. Its only purpose is to allow for easy cursor movement. I'm going to use CURSOR to allow the user to travel more easily between the two subfiles. Because both subfiles are active, the user is able to move between them with one keystroke, using either the Tab or Field Exit key.

This is important because control in a load-all subfile isn't passed back to the program when the page keys are pressed. As a result, IBM i decides which subfile to page to by interrogating (not harshly) the cursor position on the screen. If the cursor is positioned anywhere in the top subfile, the top subfile will be affected when the page keys are pressed. If the cursor is positioned in the bottom subfile, the bottom subfile will be affected. Without my CURSOR field, the user will have to use the arrow keys, and potentially many keystrokes, to maneuver between the subfiles. If the cursor is located in the HEADER or FOOTER format, the controlled subfile depends on how you coded the RPG.

That said, let's move on to the RPG.

Where's the EXFMT?

The RPG code (SFL015RG) looks much like a typical load-all subfile program, except that I'm loading and displaying two subfiles instead of one. Figure 6.5 shows the F specs for the display file. Notice that there are two subfiles defined, SFL1 and SFL2.

```
FSf1015df  cf   e              Workstn Sfile(Sfl1:Rrn1)

F                                      Sfile(Sfl2:Rrn2)

F                                      Infds(Info)
```

Figure 6.5: The F specs for the display file used in the over/under subfile method.

Up to this point, you might be accustomed to seeing a WRITE operation, which displays the function key format, and an EXFMT operation, which displays to and reads from the subfile control and record formats. The code in Figure 6.6 isn't much different. It just looks that way.

```
Write Header;      // Display the header of the screen.

Write Footer;      // Display the footer of the screen.

Write Sf2ctl;

Write Sf1ctl;

Read Sf2ctl;

Read Sf1ctl;
```

Figure 6.6: Using only WRITE statements to display subfiles.

The EXFMT operation actually performs a write, followed by a read. In my example, I want to make both subfiles active at the same time. To do this, I'm going to write them both to the screen first, and then read from both of them when the user presses Enter or a valid function key.

The rest of the RPG is very similar to what you've seen before with load-all subfiles. It isn't responsible for much because the DDS is controlling almost everything. Control is returned back to the RPG program so it can process the whole screen, and not just an individual subfile.

Anything specific to one subfile (such as paging), as determined by the cursor location, will be accomplished by the DDS. When the cursor is in a neutral spot (the header or footer), the top subfile, SF1CTL, will be paged when the user presses the page keys. This is because that's the subfile control record that was written last. Otherwise, the subfile that contains the cursor will be the one that's paged through. I've simplified the RPG to allow you to concentrate on multiple subfile concepts. In the real world, you're probably not going to load each subfile with the exact same data, unless, of course, you really want to emphasize that data.

Keep It Simple

You might be wondering whether you can display multiple self-extending or page-at-a-time subfiles on a screen. The answer is yes. However, you're going to do a lot more work in your RPG program. Instead of the DDS determining which subfile should be paged, you'll have to do that in your RPG. It's not a big deal, but it is more work. You'll have to know where the cursor was when the user pressed the Page Up or Page Down key, and process the correct subfile accordingly.

You might also have an issue if you're loading subfiles from the same data file. Maybe you're reading from a file and interrogating the data before determining which subfile to load. If you don't use the load-all technique, you're going to have fun trying to keep track of all the file pointers associated with each subfile.

Recommendation
Use load-all subfiles when you're displaying multiple subfiles on a screen.

Side-by-Side Subfiles

The other way to display multiple subfiles on a screen is side by side. Subfiles, however, cannot reside side by side on the same screen. When you define DDS for a screen that will include a subfile, you have to concern yourself with the row in which you're defining each record format. This is because the subfile control record takes up the top three or four rows of the screen in a typical subfile layout. It could be more rows, or less, but in general, the top portion of the screen is the subfile control, or header, portion. By the way, you can just as easily reserve the bottom portion of the screen for the subfile control. It doesn't have to display above the subfile record format, but it can't overlap it.

Now, back to my DDS. Once you've defined the rows the subfile control record will consume, you define the subfile record format. This is typically the middle part of the screen. It cannot overlap the subfile control record. As a result, if your subfile control header takes up rows 1 through 4, your subfile record format must start on row 5.

Finally, you usually display some sort of function key line and maybe a message line at the bottom of your screen. Again, these lines can't share the rows occupied by the subfile record format. Once you've defined which rows each format will occupy, the formats occupy every column in the row. For example, you cannot have the subfile record format using only columns 1 through 40. Even if the actual fields you define in the subfile record take up only 40 columns, the format itself consumes all the columns.

Given this information, you might be wondering how you can display side-by-side subfiles. The answer is, you can't—sort of. The only way to display subfiles side by side is to use windows. The good news is that it's easy to place windows side by side on a screen. If each of those windows happens to be a subfile window, you're now able to place subfiles side by side.

The bad news is that because these subfiles are separate windows, they cannot be active at the same time. Remember the discussion of windows in Chapter 4? You can display up to 12 windows on a screen at a time, but only one can be active at a time. However, I don't give up easily, and you shouldn't either. I'll show you a technique to make the side-by-side windowed subfiles appear as two active subfiles, side by side, on one screen.

Nothing Up My Sleeves

For this technique, I'm going to use two load-all subfile windows and place them next to each other on the screen. The complete DDS for this technique is available at *http://www.mc-store.com/5104.html* (SFL014DF). The DDS includes a header, footer, and two subfile windows.

I got fancy this time and didn't display the same data in each subfile. The first subfile contains first names and middle initials, and the second contains last names. Think of this application as a way to see how different combinations of first and last names look together.

Take a look at the subfile control record in Figure 6.7. In this example, I don't want to show the user that I'm displaying two separate windows, so I'm explicitly defining the window border as blank. Remember that the WDWBORDER keyword is optional, but if you leave it out, you'll get IBM's default border. In this case, because I want no border (based on the layout back in Figure 6.2), I use the WDWBORDER keyword to define no border.

```
A              R SF1CTL                  SFLCTL(SFL1)

A*

A                                        OVERLAY

A    32                                  SFLDSP

A                                        SFLDSPCTL

A    31                                  SFLCLR

A    90                                  SFLEND(*MORE)

A                                        SFLSIZ(0050)

A                                        SFLPAG(0010)

                                                    Continued
```

```
A                                    WINDOW(3 2 15 35)

A                                    WDWBORDER((*CHAR '          '))

A                         3  5'First Name'

A                                    DSPATR(HI)

A                         3 30'MI'

A                                    DSPATR(HI)

A          RRN1          4S 0H       SFLRCDNBR
```

Figure 6.7: The subfile control record defining a window with no border.

Both windows are defined in much the same way. The difference is in the WINDOW keyword entry in the subfile control format. Its second parameter tells you where to place (by column number) the upper-left corner of the window, as shown in Figure 6.8.

The window keywords have now been defined appropriately to place the windows side by side. Another technique I like to use with side-by-side windows is the USRRSTDSP keyword, also shown in Figure 6.8. For more on this keyword, refer back to Chapter 4.

```
A          R SF2CTL                  SFLCTL(SFL2)

A*

A                                    OVERLAY

A   42                               SFLDSP

A                                    SFLDSPCTL

A   41                               SFLCLR

A   90                               SFLEND(*MORE)

A                                    SFLSIZ(0050)

                                                      Continued
```

```
A                                    SFLPAG(0010)

A                                    WINDOW(3 41 15 35)

A                                    WDWBORDER((*CHAR '        '))

A                                    USRRSTDSP

A                            3   5'Last Name'

A                                    DSPATR(HI)

A         RRN2        4S 0H          SFLRCDNBR
```

Figure 6.8: The subfile control record for the second window.

To recap, USRRSTDSP allows you, and not the operating system, to control when your windows are saved and restored. When you use USRRSTDSP in the second window, IBM i will not save the first window when the second window is written. That's not such a big deal in this example. However, USRRSTDSP also causes the second window not to be removed when the first window is written again. Conversely, the first window isn't removed when the user toggles back to the second window.

By using the USRRSTDSP keyword and a function key to toggle back and forth between windows (F9, in this example), I can make it look as though both windows are active at the same time. The side-by-side technique still works without the USRRSTDSP keyword, but you'll see a big difference when you toggle back and forth. Without USRRSTDSP, the windows will be removed and restored, which will cause the screen to "flash" each time the toggle (F9) key is pressed. Adding USRRSTDSP to the second subfile control record makes the flash disappear, and you'll only notice cursor movement between the two windows. Try running the programs both ways to see what I'm talking about.

The Toggle Technique

The RPG program for this technique is SFL014RG at *http://www.mc-store.com/5104. html*. As usual, the program doesn't get to have much fun. The DDS is the primary controller of what happens. However, there are a few things I want to show you in the RPG that are a bit different from what you've seen before.

In the code in Figure 6.9, field WHICH_ONE, defined in the D specs, determines which subfile window to control. As the user presses F9 to toggle between windows, the WHICH_ONE field will be set to one or two.

```
DWhich_One        S              1    inz('1')
```

Figure 6.9: The WHICH_ONE field controls which subfile is made active.

The mainline code in Figure 6.10 shows how the WHICH_ONE field is used. The DOU loop, which processes the screen after I write my HEADER and FOOTER formats, displays both windows, but determines which one is active based on the WHICH_ONE field. Because I initialized this field to one in my D specs, the window on the left side will be active the first time through the loop.

```
Dou  *Inkc or *Inkl;  // Process until F3 or F12 is pressed.

  Write Header;        // Display the header of the screen.

  Write Footer;        // Display the footer of the screen.

  If Which_One = '1';  // Write the left subfile last so it is active.

    Write Sf2ctl;

    Exfmt Sf1ctl;

  Else;                // Write the right subfile last.

    Write Sf1ctl;

    Exfmt Sf2ctl;

  Endif;
```

Figure 6.10: The program determines the active subfile depending on the value of WHICH_ONE.

When the F9 toggle key is pressed, the program determines the value of WHICH_ONE. If it's one, it's changed to two; otherwise, it's changed back to one. This technique is illustrated in Figure 6.11. Upon the next iteration through the DOU loop, the value of WHICH_ONE is interrogated to determine which window will be active.

```
When Cfkey = Toggle;      // Pass control between subfiles

  If Which_One = '1';

    Which_One = '2';

    Rrn1 = Sflrrn;

  Else;

    Which_One = '1';

    Rrn2 = Sflrrn;

  Endif;
```

Figure 6.11: When F9 is pressed, the program sets the appropriate variables in preparation for displaying a window.

There's another neat little trick you can use to control side-by-side subfile windows in the toggle logic. When I determine which window is currently active so I can toggle to the other window, I can also set the RRN associated with the window that will become active. If you go back to the DDS, you'll notice that I used the SFLRCDNBR keyword and associated it with the relative record number in each subfile record. If you remember, SFLRCDNBR allows you to display a given page of the subfile based on the current relative record number.

In the RPG D specs, I retrieve the relative record number of the first subfile record on the page, as shown in Figure 6.12. I'm finally using something else from the file information data structure. In addition to the indicator that tells me which key the user pressed, I can get the relative record number of the first subfile record on the page. This allows me to remember which page was displayed when the user pressed the toggle key to go the next subfile.

```
D Sflrrn                 378     379B 0
```

Figure 6.12: Using the relative record number to mark the page when leaving one subfile and making another active.

In my toggle logic, I not only set WHICH_ONE to the appropriate value, but I also set the RRN variable (used in the SFLRCDNBR keyword) for the window that's about to be displayed as it was before it was made inactive. For example, if I page through the left subfile, ending up on page 4, and then toggle to the right subfile, I want page 4 to stay on the screen when I toggle back. Without the SFLRRN value from the file information data structure, the subfile will always revert to what it was set to in the SFLBLD routine (in this case, one). By adding this little technique, the subfile will stick to where it was when it was last active. Again, I invite you to try side-by-side subfiles with and without the SFLRRN value from the INFDS to see the difference.

Another way to retrieve the subfile relative record number from the first subfile record on the page is to use the SFLSCROLL keyword. This keyword and a five-byte zero-decimal hidden field in your DDS will provide the same information as the D spec in Figure 6.12. Figure 6.13 shows how to code the SFLSCROLL keyword. When control is passed back to your program, the RETRN field will contain the same information as that contained in SFLRRN from Figure 6.12: the relative record number of the first record on the page. If you decide to use SFLSCROLL instead of the file information data structure, note that SFLSCROLL and SFLRCDNBR can't be used on the same field. Also, SFLSCROLL can't be used if SFLPAG and SFLSIZ are equal.

```
A           RETRN         5S 0H       SFLSCROLL
```

Figure 6.13: Using SFLSCROLL to pass information back to the program.

Summary

There you have it—two ways to display multiple subfiles on a screen. The over/under technique is fairly straightforward and allows you to easily implement multiple, active subfiles on a screen using traditional subfile techniques.

Side-by-side subfiles aren't too difficult to implement, but they can't be made active at the same time. However, using a little finesse, such as a toggling technique, the USRRSTDSP keyword, and the relative record number value from the file information data structure, you can create elegant side-by-side subfiles that look to the user as if they're all active at the same time.

SUBFILES AND DATA QUEUES— A PERFECT COMBINATION

The technique you'll learn in this chapter came to me when I was asked to create a subfile application that would work like the Programming Development Manager (PDM), shown in Figure 7.1. If you've ever looked at PDM, you might have marveled at what a cool subfile application it is. PDM is extremely flexible. It allows you to move anyplace in a subfile-like panel, page forward or backward from that position, change a record on any page of the subfile, and process all changed records only when the Enter key is pressed. On their own, each of these features is simple to code in an RPG subfile program. The real fun begins, though, when you combine the features.

I worked for a software development house that wanted the IBM look-and-feel on all of its screens. The thinking was that users familiar with the AS/400 would be comfortable using the interactive screens in our software and would require less training. It seemed simple enough at first, but as you will soon see, incorporating all the features included with PDM into a subfile application is no small task. In fact, PDM isn't even a subfile application; its displays are written using the User Interface Manager (UIM), the language used for many of the system's native operating system commands and all of the help panels.

```
┌─────────────────────────────────────────────────────────────────────┐
│                    Work with Objects Using PDM              PUB1      │
│                                                                       │
│   Library . . . . .   KVANDEVER1      Position to . . . . . . . .     │
│                                       Position to type  . . . . .     │
│                                                                       │
│   Type options, press Enter.                                          │
│     2=Change        3=Copy        4=Delete     5=Display     7=Rename │
│     8=Display description          9=Save      10=Restore    11=Move …│
│                                                                       │
│   Opt  Object      Type        Attribute   Text                       │
│   _    QCLSRC      *FILE       PF-SRC       Sources CL-Programs        │
│   _    QDDSSRC     *FILE       PF-SRC       DDS-Sourcen                │
│   _    QRPGLESRC   *FILE       PF-SRC       RPG-Sourcen                │
│                                                                       │
│                                                                       │
│                                                                       │
│                                                              Bottom   │
│   Parameters or command                                               │
│   ===>                                                                │
│   F3=Exit        F4=Prompt         F5=Refresh        F6=Create        │
│   F9=Retrieve    F10=Command entry F23=More options  F24=More keys    │
│   This is a subsetted list.                                        +  │
└─────────────────────────────────────────────────────────────────────┘
```

Figure 7.1: A typical PDM screen.

The Dilemma

What do you do if you're an RPG programmer who likes the look, feel, and flexibility of PDM, but doesn't know how to obtain these features using UIM? Do you learn UIM? You could, but if you already know RPG, is learning a new language the most effective use of your time? This was the dilemma I faced.

I'm not against learning UIM, but I thought that there must be a more efficient way to get the same results using RPG and subfile processing. After some research, I recommended to my programming group that we use data queues to add the necessary flexibility to our subfile applications. Data queues are the way to get the features and flexibility you're looking for—without having to learn UIM.

Data Queues 101

Data queues are a type of system object (type *DTAQ) you can create and maintain using IBM i commands and APIs. They are IBM i objects that can be used to send and receive multiple record-like strings of data. Data may be sent to and received from a data queue from multiple programs, users, or jobs. This makes data queues an excellent mechanism for sharing data. They provide a fast means of asynchronous communication between two jobs because they use less system resources than database files, message queues, or data areas.

Data queues have the ability to attach a sender ID to each entry placed on the queue. The sender ID, an attribute of the data queue established when the queue is created, contains the qualified job name and current user profile.

Another advantage to using data queues is that you can set the length of time a job will wait for an entry before continuing its processing. A negative wait parameter tells the job to wait indefinitely for an entry before processing. A wait parameter of zero to 99,999 tells the job to wait that number of seconds before processing.

High-level language programs (HLLs) can send data to a data queue using the Send to a Data Queue (QSNDDTAQ) application programming interface (API). Similarly, HLLs can receive data using the Receive from a Data Queue (QRCVDTAQ) API. Data queues can be read in FIFO, LIFO sequence, or keyed sequence. The technique I use for building PDM-like subfile applications requires a keyed data queue. Keyed data queues allow the programmer to specify a specific order in which entries on the data queue are received, or to retrieve only data queue entries that meet a criterion. That is, the programmer can receive a data queue entry that's equal to (EQ), greater than (GT), greater than or equal to (GE), less than (LT), or less than or equal to (LE) a search key.

Why Should I Use a Data Queue in a Subfile Program?

The reason behind using data queues in a subfile program stems from a combination of user requirements and an interest in selecting the most efficient solution for that combination. I wanted to provide the PDM look-and-feel by allowing users to go anywhere in the subfile using the position-to field, and then page up or down from that new position. This is easily accomplished using a page-at-time subfile.

However, I also wanted the data that was changed on subfile records to be saved, regardless of where the user navigated in the subfile, until the user was ready to process them by pressing Enter. This is accomplished easily in a load-all or self-extending subfile, but not in a page-at-a-time subfile.

With page-at-a-time subfiles, you have to clear and build one new page of subfile records every time the user pages and uses a position-to field. Any previously changed records are not saved. I needed a way to combine the flexibility of the page-at-a-time subfile with the capability to process the changed records only when desired. I needed a place to store and reuse changed subfile records until the user was ready to process them. Using data queues to accomplish this task instead of data structures, files, or arrays freed me from some additional work.

During an interactive job, the data queue APIs can provide better response times. They also decrease the size of the program, as well as its process activation group (PAG). This, in turn, can help overall system performance. In addition, data queues allow the programmer to do less work. When you receive an entry from a data queue using the QRCVDTAQ API, it's physically removed from the data queue. You don't have to add code to deal with unnecessary entries.

I use the data queue to store a replica of the changed subfile record. Each time a subfile record is changed and the Enter or Page key is pressed, the changed subfile record is stored in the data queue. I do this because I build the subfile one page at a time, so I need to know which records were previously changed. Once records are no longer displayed on the screen, they're not part of the subfile.

When the user positions through the subfile by scrolling or by keying something in the position-to field, the program checks to see if each record read from the data file exists in the data queue before loading it to the subfile. If the record exists in the data queue, it's written to the subfile, along with the earlier changes, and marked as changed. When the user is ready to process all the changed records by pressing Enter with nothing in the position-to field, the records is processed appropriately from the data queue. I have modified my original Name Master File Maintenance application using these principles. You can check out the CL, DDS, and RPG that make this work at *http://www.mc-store.com/5104.html.*

The DDS—Same as It Ever Was

Before I get to the RPG, I need to say a few things about the DDS and CL. For this application to have the necessary flexibility, the RPG program, not IBM i, must completely control the subfile. Of course, you know what that means: the subfile page (SFLPAG) and subfile size (SFLSIZ) values must be equal.

The subfile will never contain more than one page, but, as you'll see, the program will make it appear that the subfile contains much more than one page of data. You should otherwise recognize the DDS as our Name Master File Maintenance DDS and understand what it's doing. The complete DDS is given as SFL011DF at *http://www. mc-store.com/5104.html*.

Control Language—So Little Code, So Much Control

It's important to note that even though an entry is removed from a data queue after it's received, the space containing the entry isn't. Over the long run, performance will suffer because the data queue's size will increase. For this reason, I delete and re-create the data queue each time the program is called.

Even if you build your data queues in QTEMP, as I do, it's best to delete and re-create them, in case the user calls the program more than once before signing off. Program SFL011CL accomplishes this task. Again, you can find this program at *http://www.mc-store.com/5104.html*.

Abracadabra! The Subfile's Never More Than One Page

Now that the setup issues have been covered, it's time to perform some magic. Let's start with the RPG program, which is the Name Master File Maintenance program from Chapter 4, with a few additions thrown in. Rather than spending time rehashing the basic subfile techniques you've already seen, I'll concentrate on how the program uses a data queue to make the subfile appear larger than it really is.

The program's first task is to load the subfile with one page of records (in this case, nine). This code from SFL011RG is shown in Figure 7.2.

```
For i = 1 to Sflpag;        // Load subfile with one page of data.

  Read Sfl0011f;

  If %eof;                  // If end of file is reached,

    *In90 = *On;            // set subfile end indicator on.

    Leave;                  // Leave the For loop.

  Endif;

  Option = *Blank;          // Clear each subfile record option.

  Exsr Receive_Queue;       // See if there is a record in Q first.

  Rrn1 = Rrn1 + 1;          // Increment the subfile record number.

  If Rrn1 = 1;

    Svlnam = Dblnam;        // Save the last name for page back

    Svfnam = Dbfnam;        // Save the first name for page back

  Endif;

  Write Sfl1;               // Write the data record to the subfile.

  *In74 = *Off;             // Turn of SFLNXTCHG indicator.

Endfor;
```

Figure 7.2: Loading the subfile with one page of records.

Notice that each time a record is read from the data file, the Receive_Queue subroutine is executed. For the initial subfile load, this subroutine won't accomplish anything. (I will explain this later.) However, after the initial load, the Receive_Queue subroutine plays a vital part in the subfile load routine.

Once the subfile is initially loaded and displayed, the user can do several things:

- Scroll through the subfile
- Add, change, display, or delete records
- Position the cursor in another place in the subfile
- Exit the program

The code listed in Figure 7.3 shows that no matter what the user decides to do, the Add_ Queue subroutine is executed each time the Enter key or a valid function key (other than F3 or F12) is pressed. This subroutine uses the READC op code to find changed records in the subfile and add them to the data queue using the QSNDDTAQ API.

```
    Select;                        // Process data entered by the user.


    When (Cfkey = Enter) And (Ptname <> *Blanks);

      Setll (Ptname) Sfl001lf;

      Exsr Add_Queue;        // Add any changed sub recs to dataQ.

      Exsr Build_Subfile;    // Execute the subfile build routine.

      Clear Ptname;          // Clear the position-to field.



    When (Cfkey = Enter) And (Ptname = *Blanks);

                                                        Continued
```

```
      Exsr Add_Queue;          // Add any changed sub recs to dataQ.

      Exsr Process_Subfile;   // Process options taken on the subfile.

      Setll (Svlnam:Svfnam) sfl0011f;

      Exsr Build_Subfile;      // Execute the subfile build routine.


  When (Cfkey = Rollup) And (Not *In90);

      Exsr Add_Queue;          // Add any changed sub recs to dataQ.

      Exsr Build_Subfile;      // Execute the subfile build routine.


  When Cfkey = Add;

     Mode = 'Add    ';

      Exsr Add_Queue;          // Add any changed sub recs to dataQ.

      Exsr Add_Record;         // Call the Add Record Routine.

      Setll (Dblnam) Sfl0011f;

      Exsr Build_Subfile;      // Rebuild subfile after added record..


  When (Cfkey = Rolldn) And (Not *In32);

      Exsr Add_Queue;          // Add any changed sub recs to dataQ.

      Exsr Goback;             // Scroll back one page of the subfile.

                                                        Continued
```

```
        Exsr Build_Subfile;     // Rebuild subfile after added record..




     When Cfkey = Cancel;     // Exit if F12 is pressed.

       Leave;




       Endsl;
```

Figure 7.3: Each time a valid function key other than F3 or F12 is pressed, the changed records are added to the data queue.

Table 7.1 explains the QSNDDTAQ parameters. The data queue entry will contain the option selected by the user and the key of the data file.

Table 7.1: Required QSNDDTAQ API Parameters	
Parameter	Explanation
QUEUE	Name of the data queue
LEN	Length of the data being written to the data queue
LIB	Library containing the data queue
DATA	The actual data being written to thedata queue

Figure 7.4 shows the contents of the data queue when the user types 4 next to a record, then pages down to see another page. When the user pages down, an entry is added to the data queue that consisted of the option (4) and the value in DBIDNM, which is the key to the data file, the key to the data queue, and a hidden field in the subfile.

```
                        Data Queue Display - TAA        2/02/00  12:14

  Queue: SFL011DQ    Lib: QTEMP       Nbr of Entries:    1  Seq: *KEYED
  Max Entry Length:    256  Key Length:      7  Force: *NO    Sender ID: *NO
          Text:
  Entry: 00001     Enqueue Date: 02/02/00   Enqueue Time: 12:07:36
  Posn  ....+....1....+....2....+....3....+....4....+....5....+....6....
     1  0000004                      40000004
    33  (DBIDNM as the key)          (OPTION followed by DBIDNM)
    97
   161
   225
```

Figure 7.4: The data queue after the user enters 4 in the option field and presses Page Down.

The Add_Queue subroutine, shown in Figure 7.5, keeps track of all records changed through the subfile. For example, if the user decides to delete two records on the next page after pressing 4 to delete a record on the current page, the Add_Queue subroutine sends the two changed records to the data queue before rebuilding the subfile in the Page Forward (Build_Subfile) routine. Now there are three entries in the data queue, and nothing has been deleted. The same logic holds true if the user decides to move to another part of the subfile using the position-to field.

```
Begsr Add_Queue;


Readc Sfl1;                    // Read changed records.


// Read all changed records in the subfile and

// Write each one to the data queue use the QSNDDTAQ API



Len = 256;          // Reset the length variable


Dow Not %Eof;

  Callp Send_To_DataQ(Queue:Lib:Len:Data:Keyln:Key);

  Readc Sfl1;

Enddo;



Endsr;
```

Figure 7.5: This routine writes the changed records to the data queue.

Now we can get to the details of the Receive_Queue routine, shown in Figure 7.6. This subroutine attempts to receive an entry from the keyed data queue using the same key as the record read from the database file (DBIDNM). The QRCVDTAQ API does this for you. The order is set to EQ (equal), so you will retrieve an entry only if there is one matching the record just read from the file. If the length is greater than zero (Len > 0), an entry was retrieved from the data queue. You then set on indicator 74, which conditions SFLNXTCHG in your DDS, to mark the record as changed when the subfile record is written. By doing this, subsequent READC operations will pick up the record the next time the page is processed.

```
Begsr Receive_Queue;



// Read the data Q by the unique key from the physical file to see

// if there is a saved option.  If so, display the saved option with

// the appropriate subfile record when it is next displayed.



Order = 'EQ';        // Set the order for which to retrieve records.



Callp Rcv_From_DataQ(Queue:Lib:Len:Data:Wait:Order:

                     KeyLn:Key:Sndlen:Sndr);

If Len > 0;

  *In74 = *On;       // Set on the subfile next change indicator.

Endif;



Endsr;
```

Figure 7.6: This routine removes entries from the data queue.

Table 7.2 lists the parameters for QRCVDTAQ. If a matching entry exists in the data queue, the entry in the data queue—not the data from the database file—is written to the subfile. With this, the user can page and position through the subfile and store any changed records in the data queue.

Table 7.2: Required QRCVDTAQ API Parameters for Keyed Data Queues	
Parameter	**Explanation**
QUEUE	Data queue name
LIB	Library containing the data queue
LEN	Length of entry received from the data queue
DATA	Data received from the data queue
WAIT	How long to wait for data (indefinitely, for a negative number)
ORDER	How to get the keyed data (EQ, GE, LT, etc.)
KEYLN	Length of the key to the data queue
KEY	Key field used to retrieve data
SNDLEN	Length of the sender ID information
SNDR	Sender ID information

Whenever a record is read from the file, the data queue is checked to see if that record exists. If it does, it's displayed along with the previously selected option. A user who wanted to page up to see the first page, after having selected two records for deletion on the second page, could do so. The user would see a 4 in the original record selected for deletion, and the data queue would now contain the two records from the second page.

If the user presses the Enter key and the position-to field is empty, the Add_Queue routine executes one last time to load any changes to the current page, and the Process_Subfile routine is executed. The Process_Subfile routine in this example is a little different from the one in the original Name Master File Maintenance program. This subroutine uses the RCVDTAQ API instead of READC to process all the changed records.

Remember that changed records will reside in the data queue, not the subfile, which never contains more than one page of data. By setting the key value, DBIDNM, to one, and the order to GE (greater than or equal to), you're sure to retrieve all entries in the data queue. Figure 7.7 shows the RCVDTAQ API in action in the Process_Subfile routine. This API will be run until the length (LEN) parameter is zero. That will happen when no more entries exist in the data queue.

```
Begsr Process_Subfile;


*In41 = *On;          // Set the indicator to clear the subfile.

Write Sf2ctl;         // Clear the subfile.

*In41 = *Off;         // Turn OFF the clear subfile indicator.

Rrn2 = *Zero;         // Clear the subfile record number.

Dbidnm = 1;           // Set the key for dataq to 1.

Order = 'GE';         // Set the key order to Great Than or Equal.


Dou Len = *Zero;

Callp Rcv_From_DataQ(Queue:Lib:Len:Data:Wait:Order:

                     Keyln:Key:Sndlen:Sndr);

If Len > *Zero;       // Len will be non-zero if a Q entry was read.


  Select;

    When Option = Change;   // Option 2 is entered in the subfile opt

      Eval Mode = 'Update';
```

Continued

```
     Exsr Change_Detail;    // Display the Change Detail screen.

   If (Cfkey = Exit) or (Cfkey = Cancel);

     Leave;

   Endif;



 When Option = Delete;    // Option 4 is entered in the subfile opt

   Rrn2 = Rrn2 + 1;       // Increment the subfile record number.

   Chain Dbidnm Sfl001pf;

   Write Window1;         // Write record to subfile confirmation.



 When Option = Display;   // Option 5 is entered in the subfile opt

   Eval Mode = *Blanks;

   Chain Dbidnm Sfl001pf;

   Exfmt Panel2;          // Display the Display Detail screen.

   If (Cfkey = Exit) or (Cfkey = Cancel);

     Leave;

   Endif;



   If (Cfkey = Exit) Or (Cfkey = Cancel);
```

Continued

```
        Leave;

      Endif;



    Endsl;



  Endif;



Enddo;



// If records were selected for delete (4), throw the subfile

// to screen. If enter is pressed, execute the Delete subroutine

// to physically delete the records, clear, and rebuild the subfile

// from the last deleted record (you can certainly position the

// database file wherever you want).



If Rrn2 > 0;

  Lstrrn2 = Rrn2;

  Rrn2 = 1;

  Write Fkey2;
```

Continued

```
  Exfmt Sf2ctl;

  If (Cfkey <> Exit) And (Cfkey <> Cancel);

    Exsr Delete_Record;

    Setll (Dblnam) Sfl0011f;

  Endif;

Endif;


Endsr;
```

Figure 7.7: How to process all the changed records from a subfile by going through the data queue.

Each time an entry is received, the data is run through a SELECT routine to determine which function needs to be performed. In this program, depending on the option taken, a display screen, an update screen, or a delete confirmation subfile will appear, just as it did in my earlier example.

Summary

Controlling the subfile within the RPG program and using data queues to store and retrieve changed subfile records allows you to create an extremely flexible subfile application. It will furnish your users with everything they've ever wanted in a subfile program.

The following are some points to take away from this chapter:

- The use of data queues allows you to create the following features in one subfile program:
  - Move anywhere in the subfile using the position-to feature.
  - Page forward or backward from that position.
  - Change a record on any page of the subfile.
  - Process all changed records only when the Enter key is pressed.
- The QSNDDTAQ API is used to write subfile records you want to save to the data queue.
- The RCVDTAQ API is used to retrieve the subfile records from the data queue and write back to the subfile.

CHAPTER 8

EMBEDDED SQL AND DYNAMIC SORTING SUBFILES

Other books about subfiles often include a chapter on using the Open Query File (OPNQRYF) command with subfiles. If you haven't had a chance to use OPNQRYF before, its strength lies in its ability to sort and select data in a batch environment. I've also used it with subfile programs, and it works just fine, especially if you use optimizing techniques. In my opinion, however, OPNQRYF doesn't really add anything to the subfile itself.

Whether you use physical files, logical files, or open query files, you want to do what's best to trim your data before you load your subfile. Once the subfile is loaded, the method used to sort and select the data is usually forgotten. Regardless of how you prepare your data before loading your subfile, it's just not that exciting, as far as the subfile is concerned. I'm not saying that logical files and open query files aren't exciting. For the purpose of this book, however, I want to concentrate on things that make the subfile itself more powerful, or, as in the case of data queues in the previous chapter, make the subfile appear to be something it's not.

You're probably wondering why I dedicated a chapter to *not* talking about open query files. I didn't. I'm actually getting to a point. What if you had a tool that allowed you the same selection and sorting capabilities as database files and open query files, but also added something to the subfile application itself? Wouldn't that be awesome? Well, that's just what you get with embedded Structured Query Language (SQL).

Embedding SQL into your RPG program not only allows you to sort and select the data as you want it, but also provides the user with some added power. Suppose multiple users from different departments are going to use your subfile program, but each wants to see the data in a different order. You can certainly accomplish this by including enough logical files in your program to cover every possible sorting criterion, but that might amount to a large number of logical files—especially if users want secondary and tertiary sorts. This can also create unnecessary access-path administration by the system, if all the logical files are created for this one application. Finally, it makes for an ugly subfile-build routine in your RPG program.

Another way to allow the dynamic sorting of subfiles is to use open query files. You could create one open query for each possible sort, or dynamically create the open query based on what the user wants to do. Either way, you would be passing parameters back and forth between the RPG and CL program to either build the open query file command or select which specific open query file command to use. I've experimented with the latter method, and the CL can get a bit cumbersome if you try to give users the flexibility to sort on more than one field at a time. Don't get me wrong, I love users, but that's a lot of work just to provide each of them with a different view of the same data.

If you have the SQL licensed program installed, SQL is the answer. By embedding SQL into your RPG, you can dynamically build your SELECT statement based on how the user wants to sort the data, all in one neat little subroutine. You can also use techniques that let you provide this capability very efficiently, and with a couple of minor changes, for data on other IBM i systems. Let's see how it's done.

What Is a SELECT Statement?

Before getting into how to use SQL within an RPG program, let's talk about the specific SQL statement I'm going to build. I don't intend to completely explain SQL here, but a brief discussion of the SELECT statement is in order.

In RPG, you have a number of ways to retrieve data from a data file. You can use the CHAIN operation for random access, or any one of the read operation variations, such as READ, READE, or READPE, for multiple record retrieval in some sort of loop.

In SQL, you retrieve data from a database file using the SELECT statement. The SELECT statement is used for random, as well as multiple, record retrieval. When coding the SELECT statement, you provide the fields you want to select (unlike with CHAIN and READ operations, which retrieve all the fields all the time). If you want all the fields, you use an asterisk. The field names you want (or the asterisk) are required; you have to specify them and the file you want to retrieve them from. For example, to see FIELDA and FIELDB from FILEA, you would code a SELECT statement as follows:

```
SELECT FieldA, FieldB FROM FileA
```

To get all fields from FILEA, you would code the following SELECT statement:

```
SELECT * FROM FileA
```

I plan to use a few other parameters with the SELECT statement in my example: the WHERE and ORDER BY clauses. The WHERE clause allows for filtering criteria within a SELECT. For example, suppose I want to select the last name and first name fields from a name master file, but only for the last name "Vandever." I could do the following:

```
SELECT dblnam, dbfnam FROM sfl001pf WHERE dblnam = 'Vandever'
```

The ORDER BY clause sorts the data you retrieve. For example, to sort the data retrieved with the previous SELECT by first name, I would change the code to the following:

```
SELECT dblnam, dbfnam FROM SFL001PF WHERE dblnam = 'Vandever' ORDER BY
dbfnam
```

A few other parameters can be used with the SELECT statement, but I'm not going to cover them here. The example in this chapter takes a basic SELECT statement and dynamically builds the ORDER BY clause depending on what the user does on the screen. Now, let's check out some code.

Disperse—There's Nothing to See Here

The DDS for this subfile is standard load-all fare. There's nothing new related to subfiles in it. I have coded a window record format to allow the user to select fields on which to sort. I could have made this a subfile window, but there are only four fields from which to choose, so I decided to make the selection window a regular format instead of a subfile. As usual, you can find the complete listing for this display file (SF013DF) at *http://www.mc-store.com/5104.html*. Notice that for the second chapter in a row, the RPG is at center stage.

Behind Option 14

Before digging into the RPG code, I want to talk about the compile options you'll need to make this work. First, this source member is type SQLRPGLE, not RPGLE, as in the previous examples. This tells the compiler there are going to be embedded SQL statements in this RPG code.

The command used to create a program with a SQLRPGLE-type source member is Create SQL RPG ILE Program (CRTSQLRPGI). This command will verify, validate, and, if you choose, prepare the embedded SQL statements during compile time. When using this command, you'll need to consider some compile options. Figure 8.1 shows some of the parameters you might want to experiment with when compiling SQLRPGLE source code.

```
* COMPILING. To compile this program, you will need to use options

*            that allow it to work correctly between machines.

*            These options are---

*

*                COMMIT = *NONE

*                RDB    = Machine name that you will connect to.

*                DLYPRP = *YES

*                SQLPKG = The name and library you want to use for

*                         the package. This will put the package

*                         on the RDB machine that you specify.
```

Figure 8.1: Compiling with embedded SQL is a little different than compiling with just RPG.

The Relational Database (RDB) parameter tells you which database you're using. This can be the name of your local DB2 database, or, if you're networked using Distributed Relational Database Architecture (DRDA), it can contain the name of a remote IBM i system database. If you use a remote database in the RDB parameter, you'll need to tell the compiler where to create the SQL package. You do this by entering a library and package name in the SQLPKG parameter.

The Delay Preparation (DLYPRP) parameter indicates whether you want to delay preparation of your SQL statement until the program is run. I set this to *YES because I don't want to perform redundant access-path validation. If I entered *NO in this parameter, access path validation would be performed at compile time, and again when the cursor was opened later during run time. By entering *YES, the validation is completed only at run time.

There are many other parameters in the CRTSQLRPGI command. I suggest you peruse them for yourself to see if there's anything of interest to your specific implementation of this technique.

Now that you know how to compile an RPG program containing embedded SQL, you probably would like to know how to code one. The following are the SQL steps taken in program SFL013RG:

1. Place the input SQL statement into a host variable.

2. Connect to the appropriate database—local or remote.

3. Issue a PREPARE statement to validate and prepare the dynamic SQL. If you specify DLYPRP (*YES) on the CRTSQLRPGI command, the preparation is delayed until the first time the statement is used.

4. Declare a cursor for the statement name.

5. Open the cursor (declared in step 4) that includes the name of the dynamic SELECT statement.

6. FETCH a row.

7. When end-of-data occurs, close the cursor.

8. Handle any SQL return codes that might result.

Look, Ma, No F Specs!

Well, that "no F specs" statement isn't exactly true. There is one F spec, but it's used only for the display file. There are no F specs for the data files because I will introduce them in the embedded SQL.

The subfile-related code in this program (SF013RG) should look familiar to you. It's a basic load-all subfile program used to list the names from our file. This program allows the user to display a window using the F4 key, and select a field on which to sort. When the user presses Enter after selecting a field, the data will sort by that field and be redisplayed on the screen.

The D Specs

I'll create the basis for my dynamic selection capability with the help of D specs. First, I define a stand-alone field, SELCT1, as being 500 bytes long to hold my initial SQL statement. (I selected the number 500 at random, but you need a variable large enough to hold your SQL statement.) I initialize this field with my SQL statement, as shown in Figure 8.2.

```
DSelct1           S              500A    INZ('SELECT dblnam, dbfnam, -

D                                        dbmini, dbnnam -

D                                        FROM kvandever1/sfl001pf -

D                                        ORDER BY ')



DSelct2           S              500A    INZ(' ')
```

Figure 8.2: The D specs used to build the initial SELECT statement.

I then define a second stand-alone field, SELCT2, also 500 bytes long, to hold the user-defined SQL statement. This will be made up of the initial SQL statement from SELCT1, plus the selection criteria assigned by the user. I also define a stand-alone field called ORDER and initialize it to DBLNAM, which is the name of the last name field in the database file. The ORDER variable will be used to append the field selected by the user to the ORDER BY clause in the SELCT1 variable.

Rules and Regulations

All blocks of SQL code must begin with a slash ("/") in position 7, followed by the EXEC SQL statement, and end with another slash in position 7, followed by the END-EXEC command. You place all your SQL code between the EXEC and END-EXEC commands. Each line is signified by a plus sign in position 7.

Figure 8.3 shows the first section of embedded SQL. The CONNECT RESET statement connects to the local DB2 database. If you were going to connect to a database on another machine, you would do so by replacing the RESET parameter with the name of the remote database.

```
C/EXEC SQL

C+ CONNECT RESET

C/END-EXEC
```

Figure 8.3: The embedded SQL to connect to a local database.

You've Got to Prepare, Declare, and Open

Now let's look at the rest of the mainline routine. First, I'm going to execute the PREP subroutine, shown in Figure 8.4. This is where the dynamic SQL statement will be built.

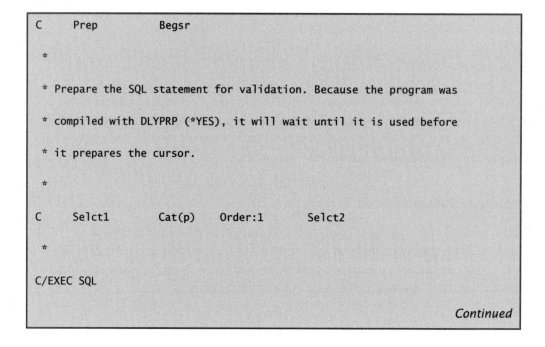

```
C       Prep            Begsr

 *

 * Prepare the SQL statement for validation. Because the program was

 * compiled with DLYPRP (*YES), it will wait until it is used before

 * it prepares the cursor.

 *

C       Selct1          Cat(p)    Order:1        Selct2

 *

C/EXEC SQL
```

Continued

```
C+    PREPARE sel FROM :selct2

C/END-EXEC

 *

 * Declare the SQL cursor to hold the data retrieved from the SELECT.

 *

C/EXEC SQL

C+ DECLARE PREMCSR SCROLL CURSOR FOR SEL

C/END-EXEC

 *

 * Open the SQL cursor.

 *

C

C/EXEC SQL

C+ OPEN PREMCSR

C/END-EXEC

 *

C                       endsr
```

Figure 8.4: The PREP subroutine prepares the SQL statement for validation.

The first thing I do is create the dynamic SQL statement based on what the user selected. Because this is the first time through, I use the default value for the ORDER variable, set in the D specs. Subsequent times through this subroutine, the user will have selected a field by which to sort the data, and that data will be placed in the ORDER variable. Once I've appended the data, in order, to the original SELECT statement defined in my D specs, I have a complete statement that will retrieve the data and order it appropriately.

Now I'm going to use that statement to retrieve my data. I use PREPARE to prepare a statement called SEL using the new SELECT2 variable I just created. This statement will validate the SQL statement contained in the SELECT2 variable. Next, I declare a cursor called MYCSR using the DECLARE statement. I am going to allow this cursor the ability to scroll. (More on this in a minute.) Finally, I open the cursor using the OPEN command.

Before I go on, let me explain cursors a little. When SQL runs a SELECT statement, the resulting rows create a result table. A cursor provides a way to access that result table. It's kind of like a subfile in its own right. The cursor is used within an SQL program to maintain a position in the result table. SQL uses the cursor to work with the data in the result table and make it available to your program. Your program may contain several cursors, although each must have a unique name.

There are two types of cursors: *serial* and *scrollable*. A serial cursor is defined without using the SCROLL keyword. This type of cursor allows you to fetch each row once, and only once. If you want to retrieve a row more than once, you need to close the cursor and reopen it. This kind of cursor is perfect for a load-all subfile because you want to see the data only once before loading it into your subfile. It's the subfile that will allow for data scrolling, in this case.

The scrollable cursor is what I've defined in Figure 8.4, even though this example involves a load-all subfile. The advantage of a scrollable cursor is that you can move back and forth throughout the rows of data. Using different parameters in a FETCH statement, you can read the next or prior row, navigate to the first or last row, read the same row over again, or position any number of rows forward or backward from the current row. This type of cursor can be used if you're building your subfile one page at a time. The data remains in the cursor and is loaded into your subfile only one page at a time.

I have validated the SELECT statement contained in the variable using the PREPARE command, created a scrollable cursor that will contain the result table from the SELECT statement using the DECLARE command, and opened the cursor using the OPEN command. We're now ready to load the subfile from the cursor.

Here, Boy! Fetch!

Take a look at Figure 8.5. Instead of loading the subfile directly from the database file, I am going to load it from the cursor, using the SQL FETCH command.

```
  Dou Sqlcod <> 0;


/End-Free

*

* Get the next row from the SQL cursor.

*

C/EXEC SQL

C+    FETCH NEXT FROM premcsr

C+       INTO :dblnam, :dbfnam, :dbmini, :dbnnam

C/END-EXEC


/Free


  If Sqlcod = 0;
```

Continued

```
   Rrn1 = Rrn1  + 1;

   Write Sfl1;

 Endif;




 Enddo;
```

Figure 8.5: Retrieving records from the cursor using the FETCH statement instead of reading from a data file.

Notice that my FETCH command is inside a DO loop. I use the FETCH NEXT command and place the results into my display-file field names. Because this is a scrollable cursor, I use the NEXT parameter. As I mentioned before, however, you don't have to use a scrollable cursor when using a load-all subfile. I did because I wanted to show you some of the parameters you can use with a scrollable cursor.

The SQLCOD variable determines whether to write to the subfile record format. If you're astute, and I know you are, you might have noticed that SQLCOD isn't defined anywhere in the program or the display file. So, where did it come from? Well, when you embed SQL in your program and use the CRTSQLRPGI command to create the program, a data structure not unlike the file information data structure is included in your program. It's filled with all sorts of information on the SQL statements embedded inside your program.

One example of that information is the error code returned when an SQL statement is run. Contained in the SQLCOD variable, it's set to zero upon successful execution of an SQL statement. For more information about the SQL Data Area (SQLDA), see the "Database > Reference > SQL Reference" topic in the IBM i Information Center.

For this program, the only data I use from the SQLDA is contained in the SQLCOD variable. Once my subfile is loaded, I'm ready to display it. Now, let's get back to the mainline code.

Let's Kick It Up a Few Notches!

When displaying the subfile the first time, you'll see the data sorted by last name. That's because I initialized the ORDER variable to the last name field. Now that the user has received the data, he or she can press F4 to sort it another way.

When F4 is pressed, the SORT subroutine is executed, which will determine what to place in the ORDER variable. Once the sort criterion is determined, the Build_Subfile routine is executed. Figure 8.6 shows what happens when F4 is pressed.

```
When Cfkey = Prompt;      // F4 key is pressed.

  Exsr Sort;              // Sort the subfile

  Exsr Build_Subfile;    // Execute the subfile build routine.
```

Figure 8.6: When F4 is pressed, this block of code calls the sort routine before loading the subfile.

Finally, let's look at the SORT subroutine, shown in Figure 8.7. There's no new, exciting subfile code in this routine. There isn't even any SQL. However, there is some code in here that's of interest.

```
Begsr Sort;



Exfmt Window1;



Select;



  When Tab1 <> *Blank;
```
Continued

```
      Order = 'dblnam';

    Clear Tab1;


  When Tab2 <> *Blank;

    Order = 'dbfnam';

    Clear Tab2;


  When Tab3 <> *Blank;

    Order = 'dbmini';

    Clear Tab3;


  When Tab4 <> *Blank;

    Order = 'dbnnam';

    Clear Tab4;


Endsl;


Exsr Clean;

Exsr Prep;


Endsr;
```

Figure 8.7: The sort routine.

This subroutine determines which field to append to the ORDER BY clause in my dynamic SQL statement. A window is displayed that lists the fields contained in the subfile. The user selects one of these fields and presses Enter. The program then determines which field was selected and places that field in the ORDER variable. Lastly, the clean and prep routines are called to prepare the SQL statement for processing. Figure 8.8 shows what the selection window looks like.

```
_SFL013RG              Dynamic Sort with Embedded SQL          2/20/11
_                                                              09:37:53


Last Name              First Name          MI    Nick Name
Anthony                Tony                A     Bill
Baker                  Ana                 C     Abc
Bilog                  Frances             X     Han Sing
Capacino               Tony                K     Knuckles
Fleischer              Jim                 R     Jimmy
Gandalf                Norm                A     Sammy
Hezikia                Ezikiel             U     Ezy
Jamison                Antwain             F     Anty
Jim                    Coker               W     Bowling Stud
Joey                   Smite               T     Fingahs
Jonas                  Steve               W     Koolaid
Jones                  Jim                 S     Jim Jones
Jones                  Lennard             C     Lenny
Kaplan                 Gabe                T     Babe
Kekke                  Kenny               K     Don't ask
Kelly                  Vandever            M     Pookie
Kent                   Craig               S     Craig
                                                         More...

F3=Exit    F4=Prompt    F12=Cancel
```

Figure 8.8: The initial display, sorted by last name.

When the user presses F4 to request a change in sort order, the screen shown in Figure 8.9 is displayed.

```
 ┌─────────────────────────────────────────────────────────────────────────┐
 │  SFL013RG            Dynamic Sort with Embedded SQL             2/20/11   │
 │ ..........................                                      09:40:47  │
 │ :   Select a sort field   :                                              │
 │ :                         :    Name          MI   Nick Name              │
 │ :  _  Last Name           :                  A    Bill                   │
 │ :  _  First Name          :                  C    Abc                    │
 │ :  1  Middle Initial      : es               X    Han Sing               │
 │ :  =  Nick Name           :                  K    Knuckles               │
 │ :                         :                  R    Jimmy                   │
 │ :                         :                  A    Sammy                   │
 │ :                         : el               U    Ezy                     │
 │ : F3=Exit    F12=Cancel   : in               F    Anty                    │
 │ :                         :                  W    Bowling Stud            │
 │ :.........................:                  T    Fingahs                 │
 │   Jonas              Steve                   W    Koolaid                 │
 │   Jones              Jim                     S    Jim Jones               │
 │   Jones              Lennard                 C    Lenny                   │
 │   Kaplan             Gabe                    T    Babe                    │
 │   Kekke              Kenny                   K    Don't ask               │
 │   Kelly              Vandever                M    Pookie                  │
 │   Kent               Craig                   S    Craig                   │
 │                                                            More...        │
 │   F3=Exit     F4=Prompt     F12=Cancel                                    │
 └─────────────────────────────────────────────────────────────────────────┘
```

Figure 8.9: The user has pressed F4 and chosen to sort by middle initial.

After the user makes a choice and presses Enter, the file will be redisplayed. As shown in Figure 8.10, it is re-sorted based on the user's selection.

```
 _SFL013RG              Dynamic Sort with Embedded SQL           2/20/11
                                                                 09:42:08

    Last Name            First Name            MI    Nick Name
    Gandalf              Norm                  A     Sammy
    Mustard              Mitchell              A     Mitch
    Anthony              Tony                  A     Bill
    Baker                Ana                   C     Abc
    Jones                Lennard               C     Lenny
    Patterson            Tony                  C     T
    Jamison              Antwain               F     Anty
    Capacino             Tony                  K     Knuckles
    Kekke                Kenny                 K     Don't ask
    Vandever             Kevin                 M     Subfile Man
    Vandever             Kalia                 M     Smiley
    Kelly                Vandever              M     Pookie
    Laut                 Kim                   O     Kimmy
    Suanzie              Lesile                Q     Leapin' Lesile
    Fleischer     ,      Jim                   R     Jimmy
    Vandever             Felicia               R     Fish
    Vandever             Corina                R     Wine Diva
                                                              More...

    F3=Exit    F4=Prompt    F12=Cancel
```

Figure 8.10: The list re-sorted by middle initial.

Pretty simple, huh? If you wanted to separate this technique from what's easily implemented using logical files and open query files, you could allow the user to select more than one field. For example, to sort by first name, last name, and nickname, you could allow the user to type a 1 next to first name, a 2 next to last name, and a 3 next to nickname. You'd then place logic in your SORT routine to interrogate all the fields selected, place them in the correct order, and place that information in the ORDER variable. Instead of the ORDER variable containing one field to append to the ORDER BY clause, it would contain three.

What a slick technique! No open query files, and no access paths to maintain.

Summary

You've just seen how to use embedded SQL and subfiles to select and sort data dynamically. This chapter wasn't meant to fully explain SQL and SQL programming. Rather, it was intended to introduce embedded SQL to you and show how it can be used to work with subfiles. As you've seen, you can create a very flexible subfile and an efficient application, while creating an easily maintainable program.

If you're interested in learning more about SQL programming, I suggest you dig into the "Database > Programming > SQL Programming" topic in the IBM i Information Center (*http://publib.boulder.ibm.com/iseries*). You'll learn all sorts of advanced techniques, such as allocating storage and loading the SQLDA using the SQL DESCRIBE command, as well as implementing optimizing techniques to make your programs scream. Combining embedded SQL and subfile programming will enable you to take your applications to new heights. Enjoy.

CHAPTER 9

NO AVERSION TO RECURSION

U p to this point, you've learned how to display, modify, add, and delete data from database files using subfile applications. The techniques in this book work very well for independent data records, such as those in the name master file used in our example applications. With independent data records, every record exists independently of every other record in the file.

As you probably already know, data in the real world doesn't nicely conform to a straightforward, independent database file. Sometimes, data from a file can mean different things depending on how it's read. Files containing a company's organizational structure or components for manufacturing parts are often stored in awkwardly. These files tend to be stored hierarchically, making them difficult to organize in a subfile application. This chapter will show you how to use ILE and RPG IV to easily display hierarchical data in a subfile application.

ILE and RPG IV forced us (in a good way) to change the way we'd thought about designing applications. The subprocedure is a RPG feature that has opened our minds this way. You might ask, "Why the subprocedure? What happened to the procedure?" Well, in V3R1 ILE RPG, you had the ability to write one procedure per module, and that procedure was considered the main procedure. Since V3R2 (CISC) and V3R6 (RISC), you're allowed to define more than one procedure per module. You can have from zero to one main procedure, and zero to many subprocedures. Subprocedures allow a module to have multiple entry points.

For example, you might have a pricing module with many specific pricing subprocedures, each accomplishing a different pricing task. Programs outside this module now have the ability to call any or all of the pricing subprocedures contained in that module. Subprocedures allow you to better separate, organize, and reuse your RPG code without the performance impact of traditional program calls. They're different from main procedures in that they don't load a bunch of extra code that you won't use. For example, when you code a main procedure, which is in essence any RPG program you write, the RPG logic cycle code is loaded, even if you don't use it. In fact, a subprocedure can't even load the RPG logic cycle. (I can almost hear the non-cycle advocates cheering.)

This book obviously isn't intended to provide you an in-depth look at subprocedures. For that, I recommend IBM's *ILE RPG Programmers Guide* (SC09-2507) or *Programming in RPG IV, 4th Edition* by Bryan Meyers and Jim Buck (MC Press, 2010). However, to give you a better understanding of subprocedures, a summary of the benefits is in order here.

Getting to Know Subprocedures

This isn't your father's RPG. Here are a few of the specifics about subprocedures that you'll find important as you implement them in your programs:

- Subprocedures support local variables. That's right, local variables. Whatever is defined inside the subprocedure is visible only to that subprocedure. Think of the possibilities!
- Parameters can be passed by reference (as parameters are normally passed between programs), by value, or by read-only reference. Passing a parameter by value protects that parameter from being changed. Passing a parameter by read-only reference is much like passing by value because the data cannot be modified. That they can be passed by reference, though, is an added benefit.
- Variable-length and optional parameters can be defined and passed (or not passed, in the case of optional parameters).
- A subprocedure is prototyped. This permits the parameters to be checked at compile time instead of at run time, allowing for more stable applications.

- Subprocedures can be exported so they're available for use by other modules. Imagine that—write once, use many times.
- Subprocedures are called using the CALLP operation code, but they can also be used as expressions, just as you would use built-in functions, to return a value.
- Last but certainly not least, subprocedures support recursive calls. I didn't believe this at first, either, but it's true. In fact, it's this feature of subprocedures that brings me to my connection to subfiles. (It took a while to get there, but it's worth it, as you'll see.)

The Org Chart

A recursive call is generated when a subprocedure calls itself, or calls another procedure, which in turn calls the subprocedure again. Get that? Each recursive call creates another entry on the invocation stack, with new storage allocation. But beware—it's easy to start chewing up system resources.

So, when is it appropriate to use recursion? More specifically, when is it appropriate to use recursion with subfiles? If you have studied C programming, you have probably programmed a recursive call to calculate factorials. You remember factorials, don't you? The factorial of 5 (written as "5!"), is $5 \times 4 \times 3 \times 2 \times 1$, or 120. I remember coding a C program that would allow me to type a number on the command line and get its factorial. I accomplished this using recursive calls.

Such a programming exercise might be fine in school, but you're probably interested in a real-life business reason to employ recursive calls. The best time to take advantage of recursion is when your data is stored in a hierarchical level, as opposed to the relational level we're accustomed to. In a relational database, you have a parent/child relationship. That is, you have a master file, which has a one-to-many relationship with detail records contained in a detail file. As RPG programmers, we're pretty adept at displaying or printing information stored in a relational database.

A hierarchical structure (also known as a recursive structure) doesn't have this parent/child relationship. In this structure, the data is independent of the rest of the data, while also possibly being associated with it. This is true in a company's chain of command.

A person might be a manager or supervisor of other managers or supervisors, while also reporting to a manager or supervisor. That person would be listed in the hierarchy as both a manager and a subordinate.

Using a relational database system, it would be difficult to list the chain of command starting with person *X*. It wouldn't be too hard to find out who reports to person *X*, but what if I wanted to list the person who reports to the person who reports to person *X*? And what about the person who reports to the person who reports to the person who reports to person *X*? How do you know how many levels to go?

You can start to picture the subfile build routine already, can't you? Because this data is stored in a recursive fashion, it makes sense to use a recursive method to display it. So, that's what I'm going to do. I'll pass an employee's ID number and list that person's chain of command with recursive calls to the subfile load procedure. I'll mark each new level of command by indenting the names. Figure 9.1 shows what the displayed data will look like.

I'm going to CHAIN to the SFL002PF file to get an employee's subordinate. After displaying the subordinate, I'll check to see if that employee has a subordinate by calling the same procedure again, recursively. I'll drill down through the subordinate tree until I get to the last level in the chain of command—you know, the ones who do all the work. The code will then go back through the recursive calls to check each level in the tree until finally returning to the first level, where it will read the next record and, if necessary, start all over again.

Let's take a look at the code to get a better picture of what's happening.

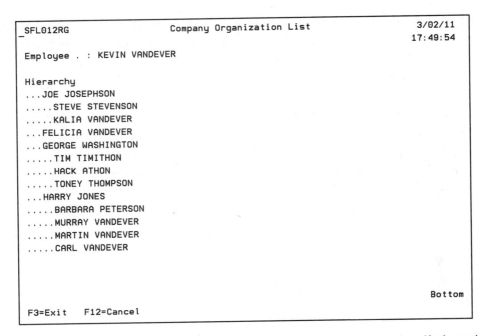

Figure 9.1: This list shows that Joe, Felicia, George, and Harry report directly to Kevin, and that Joe, George, and Harry each have direct reports.

One Field Is Worth 1,000 Bytes . . . Okay, 60

The DDS is of typical load-all nature. The only interesting thing here (other than the inherently interesting subfile specifications) is the 60-byte field, SUBNAM, listed in the subfile record format and shown in Figure 9.2. You can find the complete DDS (SFL012DF) at *http://www.mc-store.com/5104.html*.

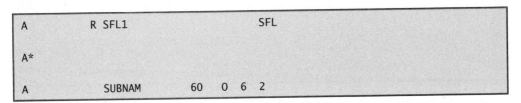

Figure 9.2: Defining a field for concatenating and indenting a name.

A field of this size allows me to concatenate the first and last name, and indent it to the appropriate level within the chain of command. By using one long field name, I can indent the name a little more to the right for each level in the chain, without knowing how many levels actually exist.

In my example, you're limited in the number of levels you can go by the number of positions available on the display screen—you can only indent so far to the right. However, you could add a field to the subfile called LEVEL and show the level of command followed by the name, without indenting and without the one long field name. I chose to indent the names to further illustrate the effect of recursive calls.

RPG (Recursion, Procedures, and Greek?)

Close the Greek-to-English translation book. This isn't Greek. It's good old RPG. Well, maybe it's not so old, but it is good and it is RPG. The example in this chapter (SFL012RG at *http://www.mc-store.com/5104.html*) is of a subprocedure that calls itself to build a subfile.

Before we dig into it, I want to mention some compile options and a couple of ways you can define them. Figure 9.3 shows how to compile this module.

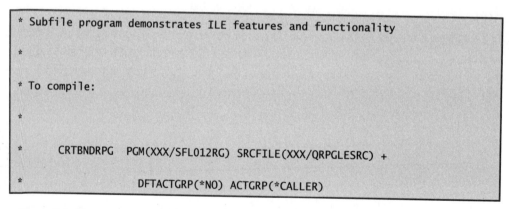

```
* Subfile program demonstrates ILE features and functionality

*

* To compile:

*

*     CRTBNDRPG  PGM(XXX/SFL012RG) SRCFILE(XXX/QRPGLESRC) +

*                    DFTACTGRP(*NO) ACTGRP(*CALLER)
```

Figure 9.3: The compilation command for this module.

When using ILE concepts such as subprocedures, you're not allowed to use the default activation group. Therefore, you must specify that you won't use the default activation group by using DFTACTGRP *NO in the option parameter. Additionally, you might want to specify an activation group. If you don't, you'll probably use QILE. I like to use *CALLER, which uses the activation group of the person calling the program. I don't want to say much here, except that using *NEW is very bad as far as performance goes. I would stick with *CALLER unless you have specific, predefined (named) activation groups—in which case you could use them. If you don't know what activation groups are or you aren't sure how to use them properly, you might want to obtain information on them before using this technique. You can get that information from the aforementioned IBM manuals.

Another technique you can use to change or override the compile options is to define them in the header specification (H spec). Remember the H spec? You probably thought it left with RPG II, but it didn't. In fact, it's more powerful than ever. For example, I could tell the compiler that I wanted source statement debugging, *SRCSTMT, and that I didn't want to generate I/O breakpoints, *NODEBUGIO. I would simply enter them in the H spec as follows:

```
H OPTION(*SRCSTMT *NODEBUGIO)
```

As an alternative, these parameters could have been entered during compilation, using the OPTION keyword in the CRTBNDRPG command. This might come in handy if you have strict default compile parameters in your shop, but need specific compile options for your program. You can easily define them in the H spec.

Proper Prototyping Promotes Predictable Parameters

For the most part, the F and D specs look pretty normal. I'm using two data files in this example: the name master file we've been using all along in this book, and a new subordinate file, SFL002PF. The subordinate file contains two fields per record: the employee ID and a subordinate ID.

I'm going to use one subfile to display the records. I'll include my usual information data structure to contain the key that was pressed by the user. There's something new to look at here, though. The last set of D specs, shown in Figure 9.4, defines a prototype for the subprocedure I'm going to use.

```
 * Prototype for NextLevel procedure: Receives two parameters

D NextLevel       pr

D   Level                     3  0 value

D   Employee                  7s 0 value
```

Figure 9.4: Prototyping defines the parameters and the optional return value of the subprocedure.

As mentioned earlier, prototyping a subprocedure allows the parameter to be validated at compile time instead of run time. To prototype a subprocedure, start with the name (NEXTLEVEL, in this case) and PR in positions 24 and 25 of the first D spec. Optionally, you can define the specifications of a return value on this line. (Remember that subprocedures can return a value.) In this example, I'm not using a return value, so none is defined.

The next two lines of my prototype are simply the parameter definitions. I'm going to pass the level and an employee ID to the subprocedure. Notice the keyword VALUE in both instances. Because I want to pass these values along, but don't want the subprocedure to have the ability to change them, I pass them by value. RPG programmers are accustomed to passing parameters by reference, which allows us to manipulate them. In this case, I don't want to manipulate the parameters. I just want to read their values.

That's it. Your subprocedure is prototyped.

CALLP Versus EXSR

Now, let's get into the code a little. The mainline routine accepts the employee ID from the user who's calling the program. It then gets the name associated with that ID and formats it for display in the heading. If the employee ID isn't found, I state so in the NAME field and display the screen. If the ID is found and formatted for display, I'm ready to start building my subfile. Figure 9.5 is the mainline code that does just that.

```
Exsr  Clear_Subfile;

  CallpNextLevel(1 :In_Employee);

  *In90 = *On;

  If Rrn1 = 0;

    *In32 = *On;

  Endif;

Endif;
```

Figure 9.5: After the subfile is cleared, the NEXTLEVEL subprocedure is called to load the subfile.

First, I execute the Clear_Subfile routine. As you guessed, it clears my subfile and gets it ready for loading. Next, I call the NEXTLEVEL subprocedure using the CALLP operation. Notice the difference in syntax between the CALLP and the traditional CALL. The parameters are passed in the CALLP by placing them inside parentheses and separating them with colons. In this case, I'm passing the level, which is 1 the first time through, and the employee ID that was passed in by the user.

Remember the prototype? It's important to note that my parameters must match by data type, not by variable name. It doesn't matter if you send constants, fields, or expressions, as long as they match the data types defined in the prototype.

This one call to the NEXTLEVEL subprocedure will start the recursive process and build the subfile. Think of it as the subfile build routine you've seen throughout this book. Although the internals of the subfile build routine are quite different from that of the NEXTLEVEL subprocedure, as far as your mainline routine is concerned, they're the same. That is, you're going to call the NEXTLEVEL subprocedure, and when control returns back to the mainline, your subfile is ready to be displayed.

After the call to the subprocedure, I set on my SFLEND indicator, *IN90. Then I check to see if any records were written to the subfile and execute the DO loop to display the subfile. Again, this isn't much different from the subfile program mainline routines throughout this book, with the exception of the CALLP versus the EXSR.

Now the fun begins. Let's take a look at how to drill down through the chain of command by using a recursive subprocedure. The subprocedure in program SFL012RG (NEXTLEVEL) is a type of Build_Subfile routine, which you've seen in previous chapters. That is, its purpose is to build the subfile. This subprocedure, however, works quite differently from what you've seen before.

The P Spec

Let's start our dissection of this subprocedure with the Procedure specification (P spec). The P spec's only purposes are to begin and end a subprocedure. The first and last lines of a subprocedure will always be P specs. The beginning of a subprocedure is denoted by a P spec containing the name of the subprocedure, followed by a "B" in position 24. The end of the subprocedure is marked by a P spec containing an "E" in position 24. Figure 9.6 shows the P specs from NEXTLEVEL.

```
 * Begin subprocedure NextLevel

P NextLevel        B

   .

   .

   .


 * End the procedure

P                  E
```

Figure 9.6: The beginning and ending P specs for the NEXTLEVEL procedure.

Variables Close to Home

The next thing you'll see in a subprocedure is the procedure interface, defined by
D specs. Each subprocedure will contain its own D specs, housing at least one
procedure interface. The procedure interface is signified by PI in positions 24 and 25,
as shown in Figure 9.7. Its purpose is to define the parameters of the subprocedure,
and it must match the prototype defined earlier. You could say it is used to "interface"
between the subprocedure and its prototype.

```
* Procedure interface. Describes procedure parameters.

* VALUE keyword causes parameters to be passed by value, not reference.

D                 pi

D   Level                    3  0 value

D   Employee                 7s 0 value



*

* Local variables - visible only within this subprocedure.

D SaveSubord      s                   like(employ)
```

Figure 9.7: D specs for the NEXTLEVEL procedure.

Following the procedure interface, you can define any local variables you want to use
in this subprocedure. Any variables you define inside the subprocedure are available
only within the subprocedure. In my example, I define a variable (SAVESUBORD) to
save the subordinate number for return from recursive calls. In addition, any local
variables that are defined are local to the specific running of a subprocedure. Any
subsequent calls to the same subprocedure (that would be recursion) will create new
local variables scoped to that instance of the subprocedure.

Submerging Subfiles into Subprocedures

Let's build the subfile. Each recursive call to a subprocedure represents a new level in the chain of command. As you can see in Figure 9.8, the structure of my subprocedure is built around a DOW loop that finds all the subordinates for the employee ID passed as a parameter to the subprocedure. Once the record is found, it's formatted using a couple of EVAL statements. The first EVAL simply fills SUBNAM with the period ("."). The second EVAL uses the %SUBST built-in function, concatenates the first and last names, and indents the concatenated name according to the level of command it's processing.

After each successful write to the subfile within the DOW loop, the NEXTLEVEL procedure is called again, passing the current level plus one and the subordinate's ID, obtained with the previous read to SFL002PF. This allows me to determine if the subordinate has any subordinate entries in the file before reading the next record for the current employee.

```
Dow Not %Eof;               // Read until no more matching emp records

   Chain SubordSfl001pf;

   If Not %Found;

     Subnam = *Blanks;

     Subnam = 'Employee information not found';

   Else;



// Fill the subnam subfile field with '...................'

// Use %TRIM BIF to strip leading and trailing spaces from database fields.
```

Continued

```
// Assign INTO the subnam field through the %subst function,

// indenting from the current level.


    Subnam = *all'.';

    %Subst(subnam : 2*(Level+1)) = %trim(dbfnam)+ ' '

                                  + %trim(dblnam);

    Rrn1 = Rrn1 + 1;

    Write Sfl1;

  Endif;



// Save the subordinate in the local variable, and recursively

// call NextLevel, updating the level number, and passing the

// current subordinate as the input employee.


  SaveSubord = Subord;

  Callp NextLevel(Level + 1 : Subord);

  Setgt (Employee : SaveSubord) Sfl002pf;  // Get next subordinate

  Reade Employee Sfl002pf;                  // for current employee.
Enddo;
```

Figure 9.8: The DOW loop within subprocedure NEXTLEVEL with a recursive call to itself to build the subfile.

Only when I come back from one or more recursive calls to the NEXTLEVEL subprocedure will I find the next direct subordinate for the current employee. I do this using the current employee (EMPLOYEE) and the last subordinate used before the call to NEXTLEVEL (SAVSUBORD). Each subsequent call to NEXTLEVEL will have the employee passed to it. The subordinate in one level of the NEXTLEVEL subprocedure becomes the employee when passed in the next call to NEXTLEVEL.

This might seem a little confusing at first. However, if you look at one instance of a subprocedure at a time, and realize that it's building the subfile for one level of the chain, you can start to understand how each subsequent call works. It's simply our SFLBLD routine with a little twist . . . and another . . . and another. . . .

Warning
Each recursive call to a subprocedure creates a new invocation of that subprocedure, and with it, automatic storage for the local data items. Because of this, infinite recursion could quickly chew up system resources. Make sure your subprocedure has some condition to stop it from calling itself infinitely. In my example, the data file ensures that the subprocedure will eventually stop calling itself. As you use this technique, make sure to condition your subprocedure so it won't get into an infinite recursive call loop. That would be bad.

Summary

This chapter is less about subfiles themselves and more about how to use subfiles with subprocedures in RPG. The following are the high-level points you should take away from this chapter:

- Subprocedures support local variables. Whatever is defined inside the subprocedure is visible only to that subprocedure.
- Parameters can be passed by reference (as parameters are normally passed between programs), by value, or by read-only reference.
- Variable-length and optional parameters can be defined and passed (or not passed, in the case of optional parameters).

- A subprocedure is prototyped. This allows the parameters to be checked at compile time instead of at run time.
- Subprocedures can be exported so they're available for use by other modules.
- Subprocedures are called using the CALLP operation code, but they can also be used as expressions, just as you would use built-in functions, to return a value.
- Subprocedures support recursive calls.

Well, that's a wrap. If you've read this book from front to back, you've come a long way from your first subfile program to the advanced techniques presented in the last few chapters. This book is also to be used as a reference, to come back to when you need a refresher on the ways of the subfile.

My intent has been to give you the tools necessary to provide your customers and user communities with flexible, efficient, and effective subfile applications. I also hope I've helped you, as a programmer, stretch your imagination as to how subfiles can be deployed. Take what you've learned here and go do great things!

INDEX

Note: **Boldface** numbers indicate code; *t* indicates a table.